PAINTO LAB

THE GREAT GEOMETER

VOLUME: 1

Copyright © 2020 by **Painto Lab**

All rights reserved. No part of this book may be reproduced or used in any manner without written permission of the copyright owner except for the use of quotations in a book review and certain other non-commercial uses permitted by copyright law.

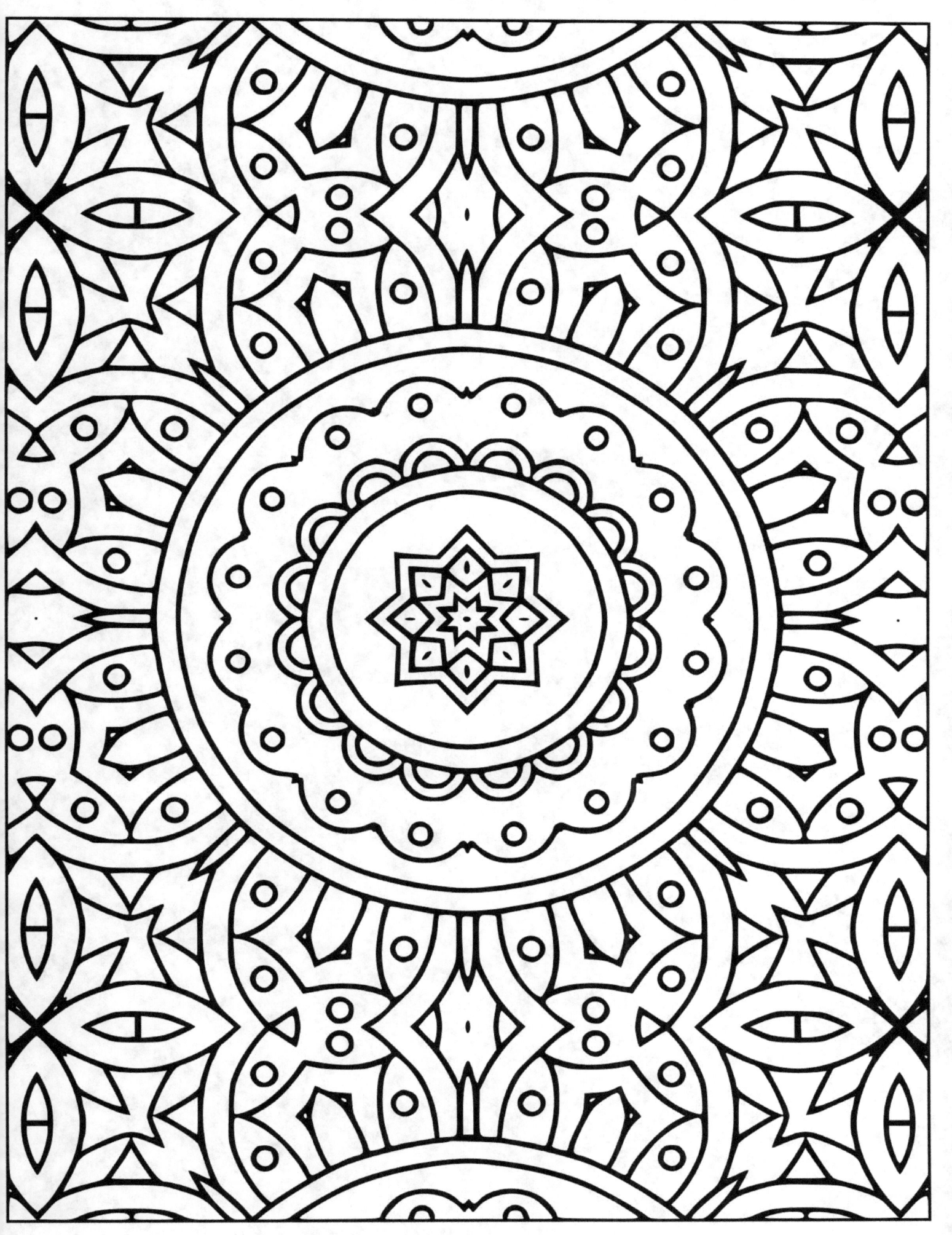

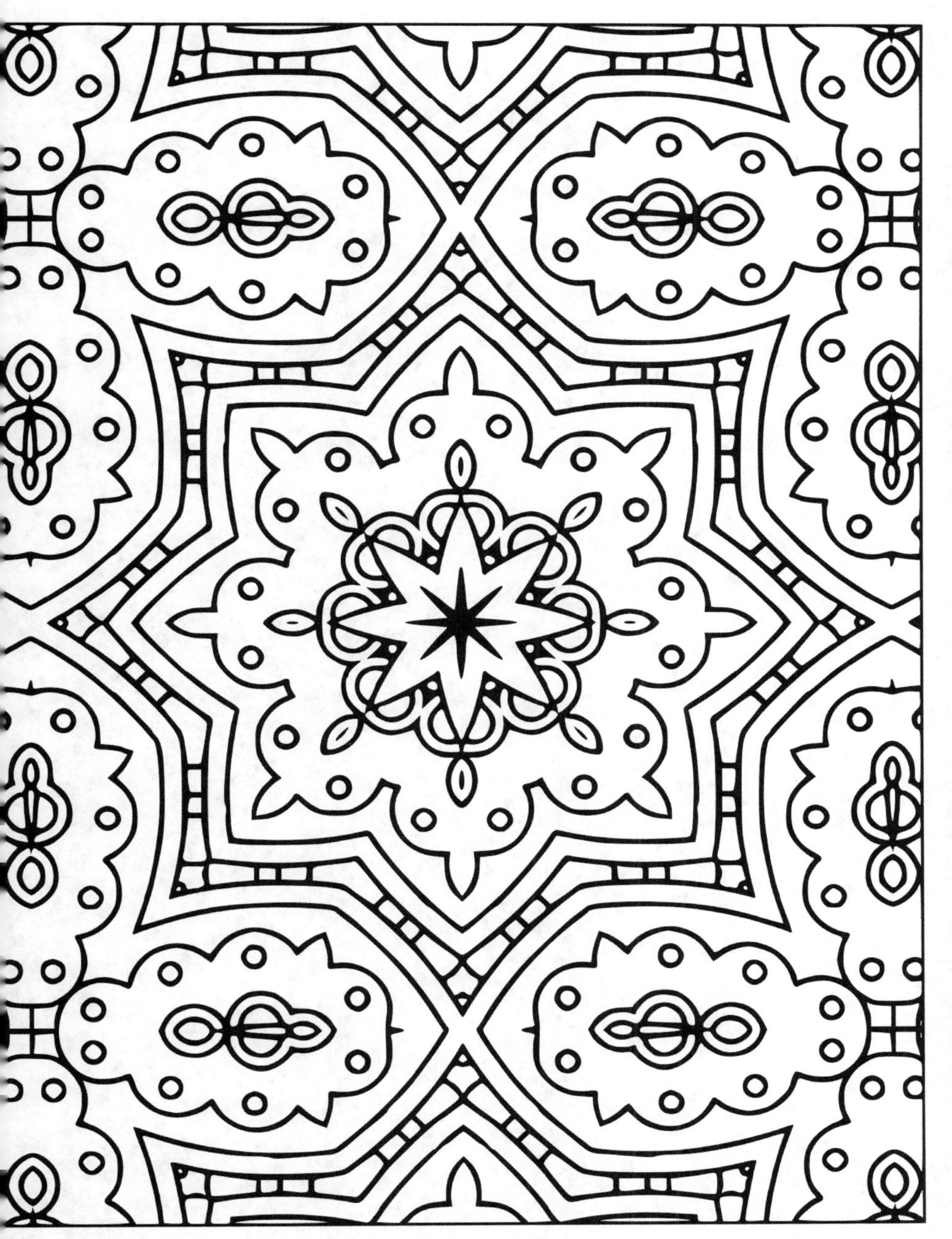

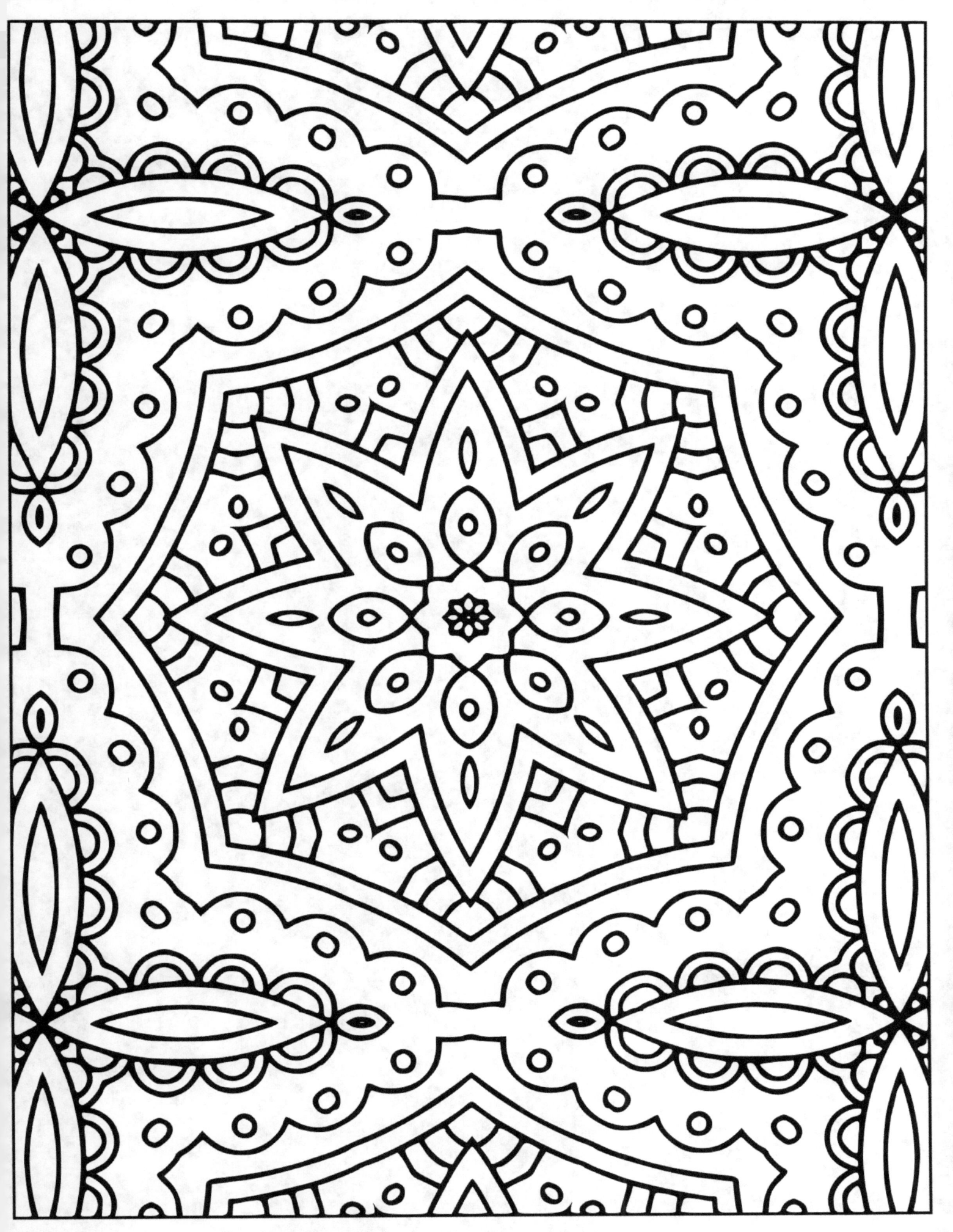

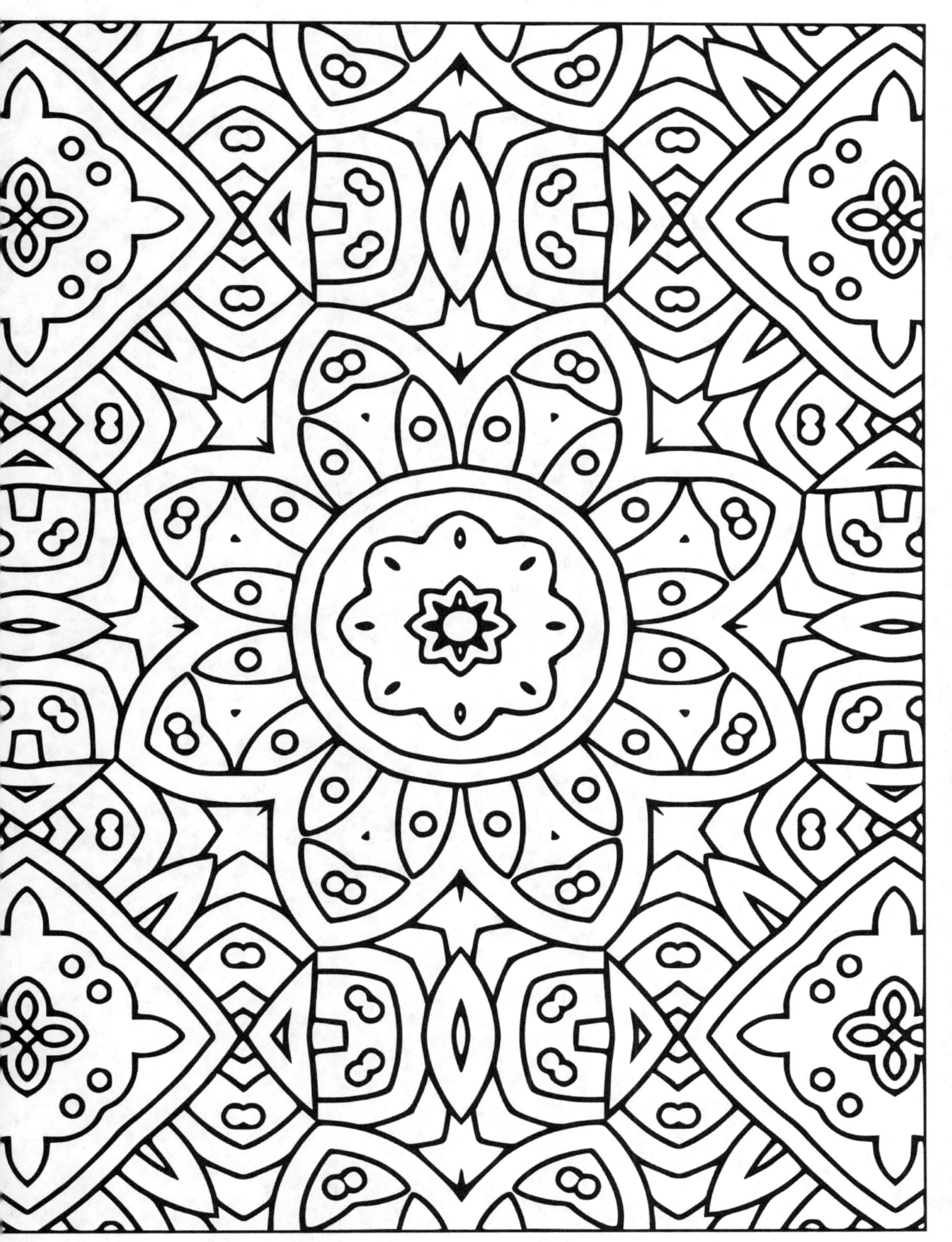

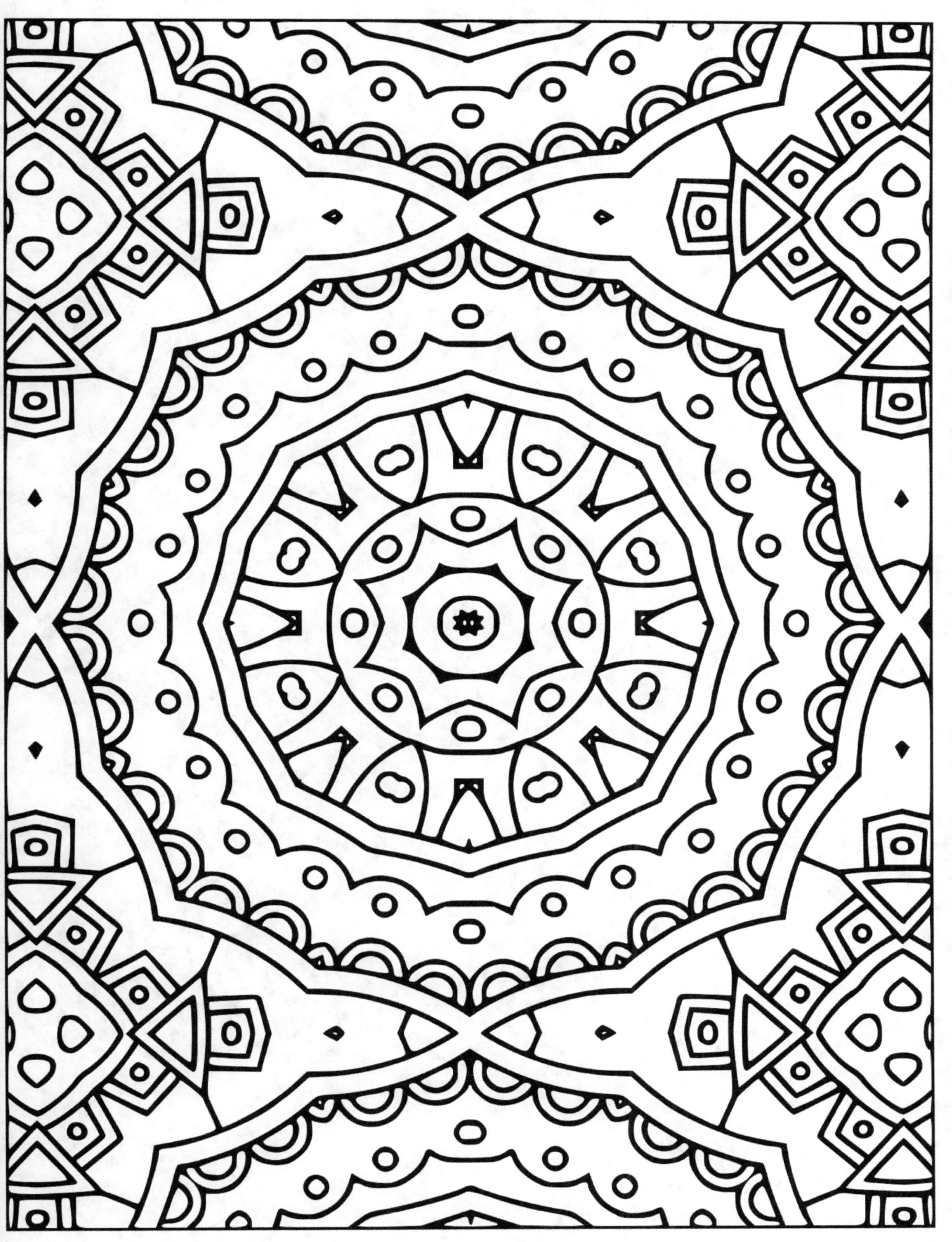

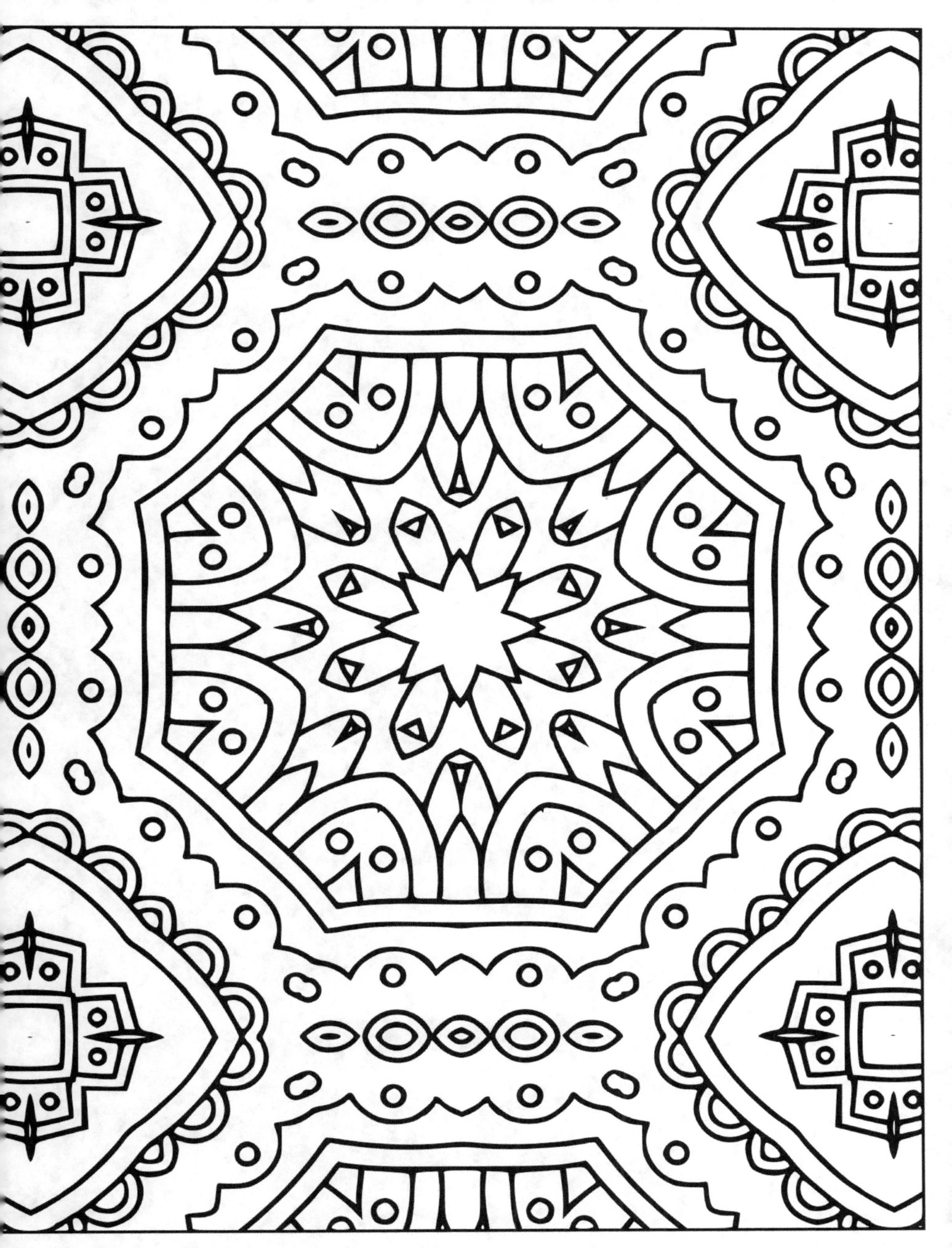

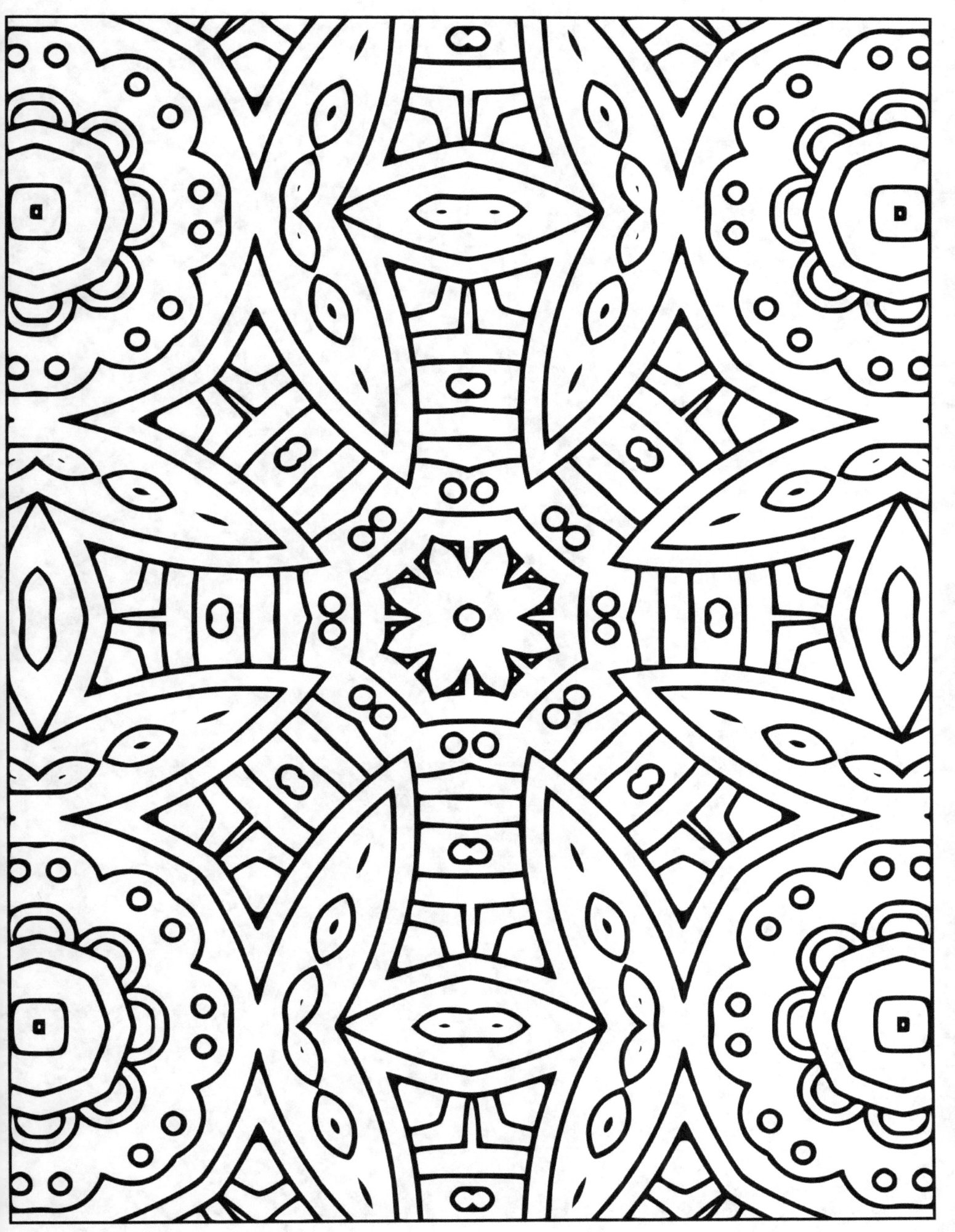

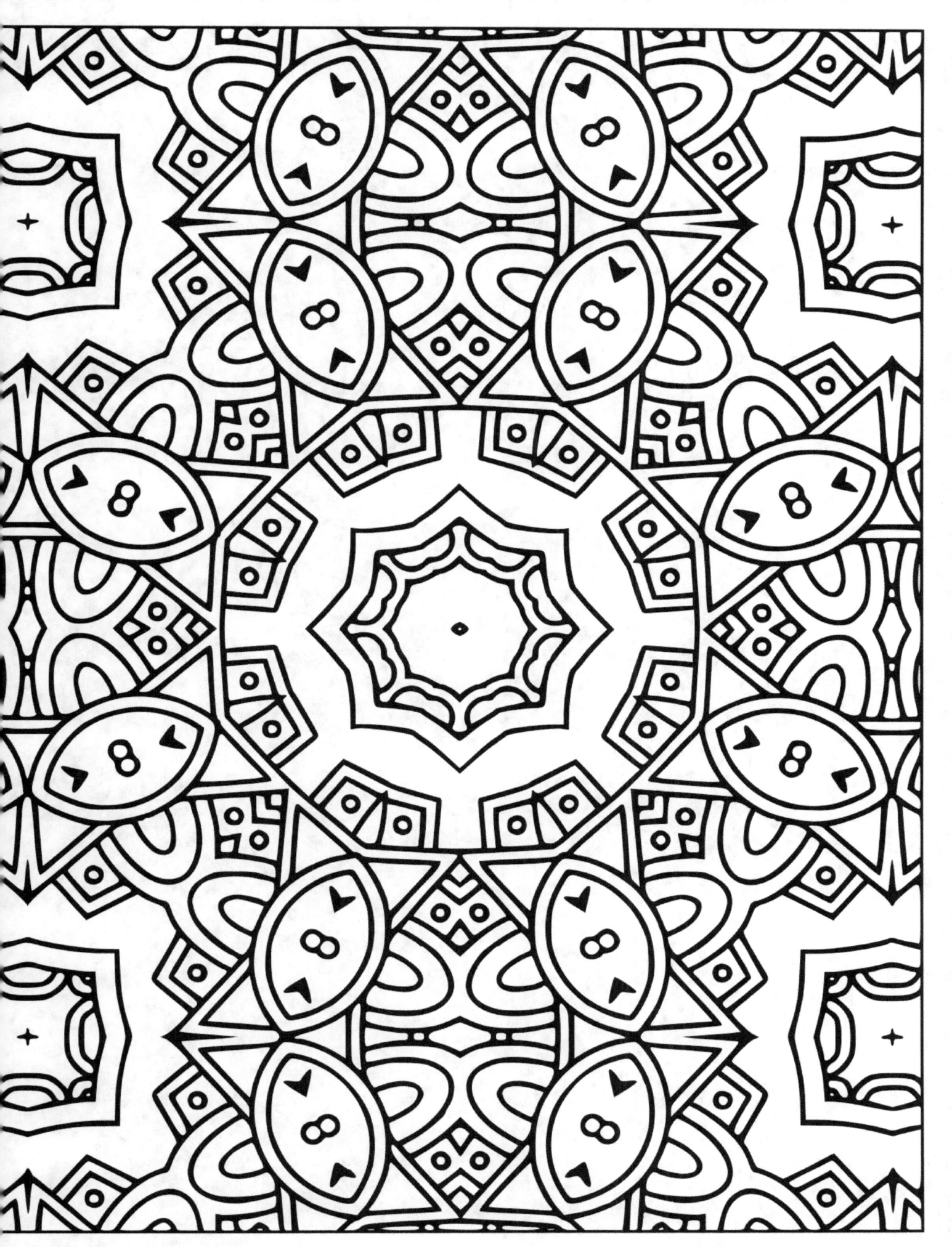

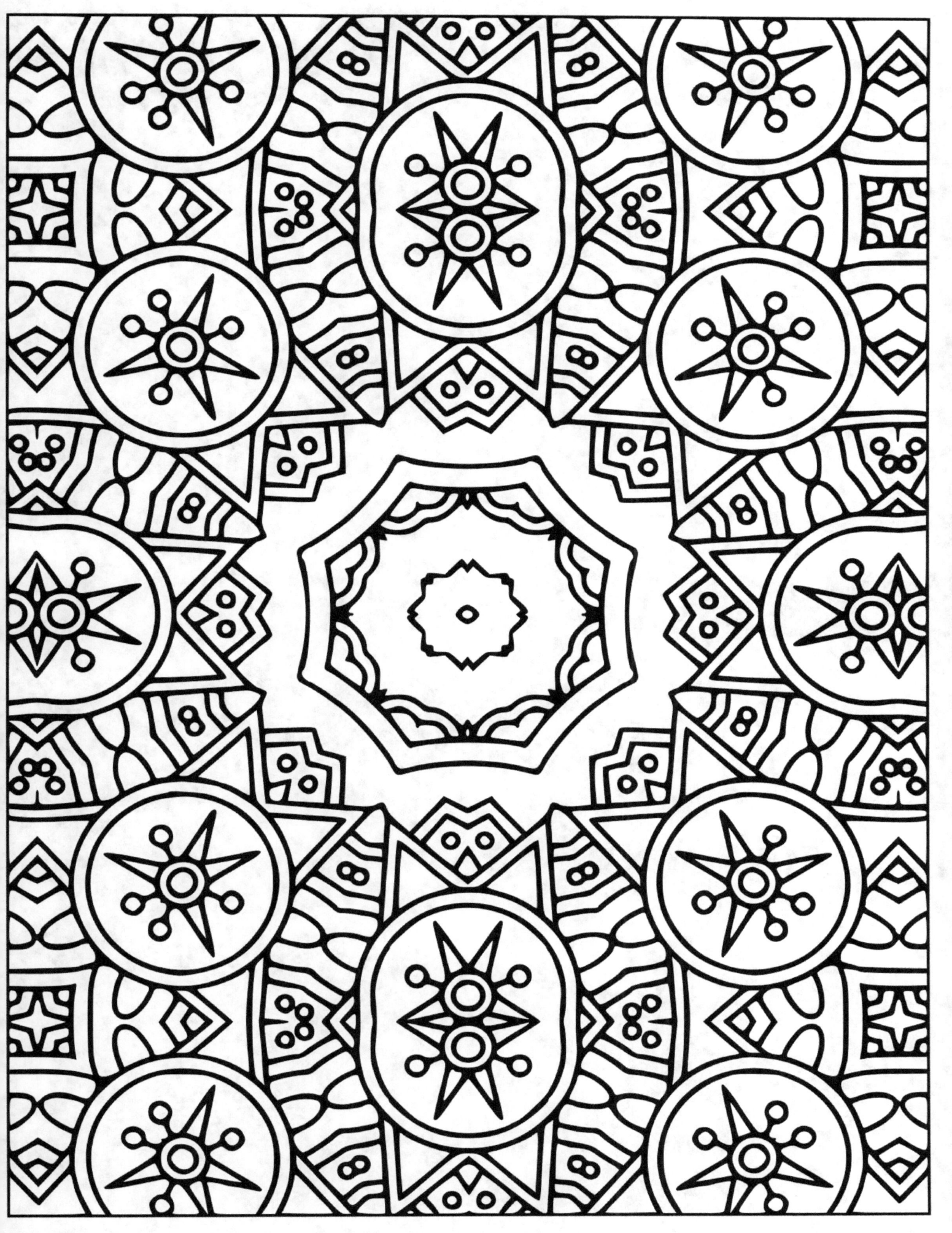

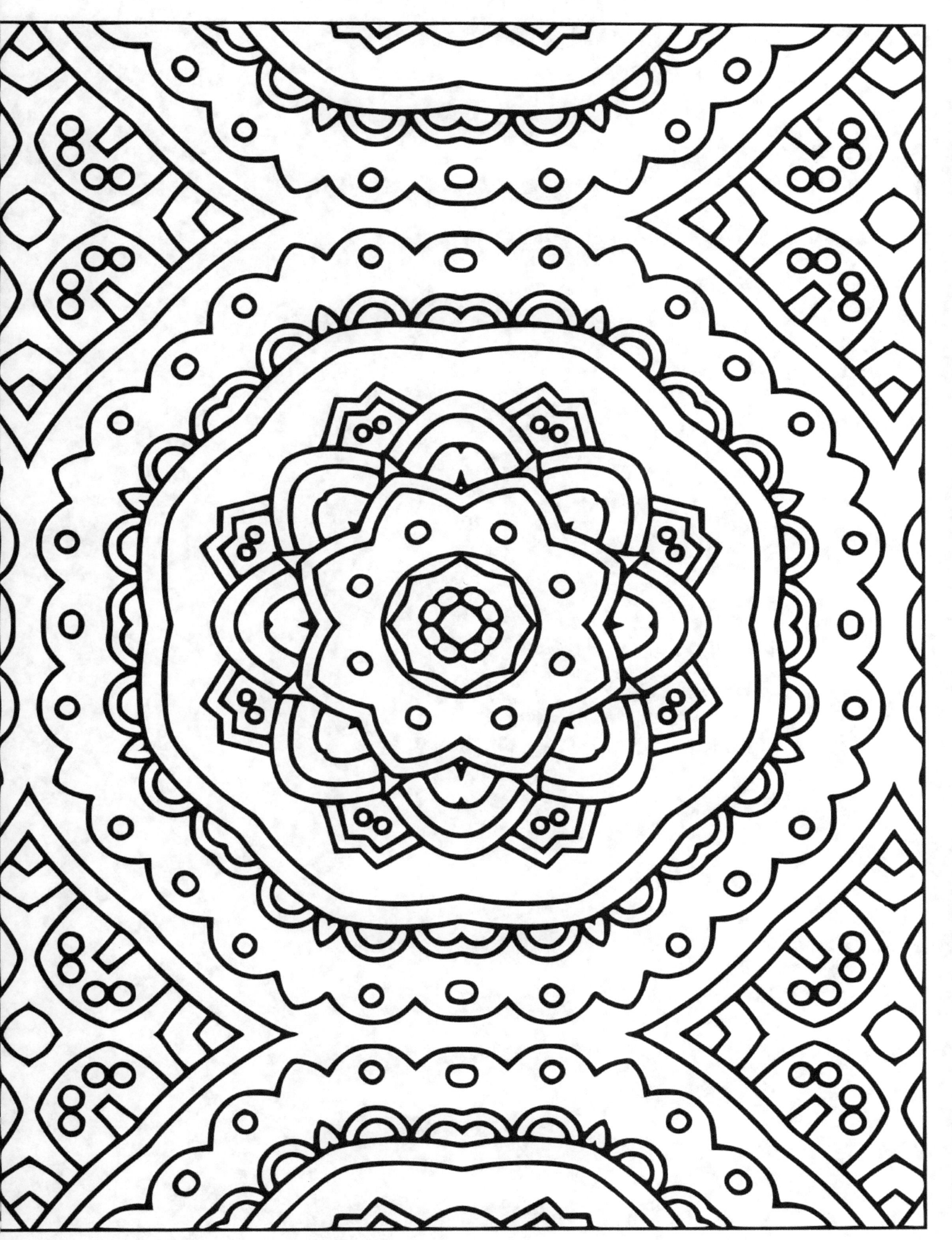

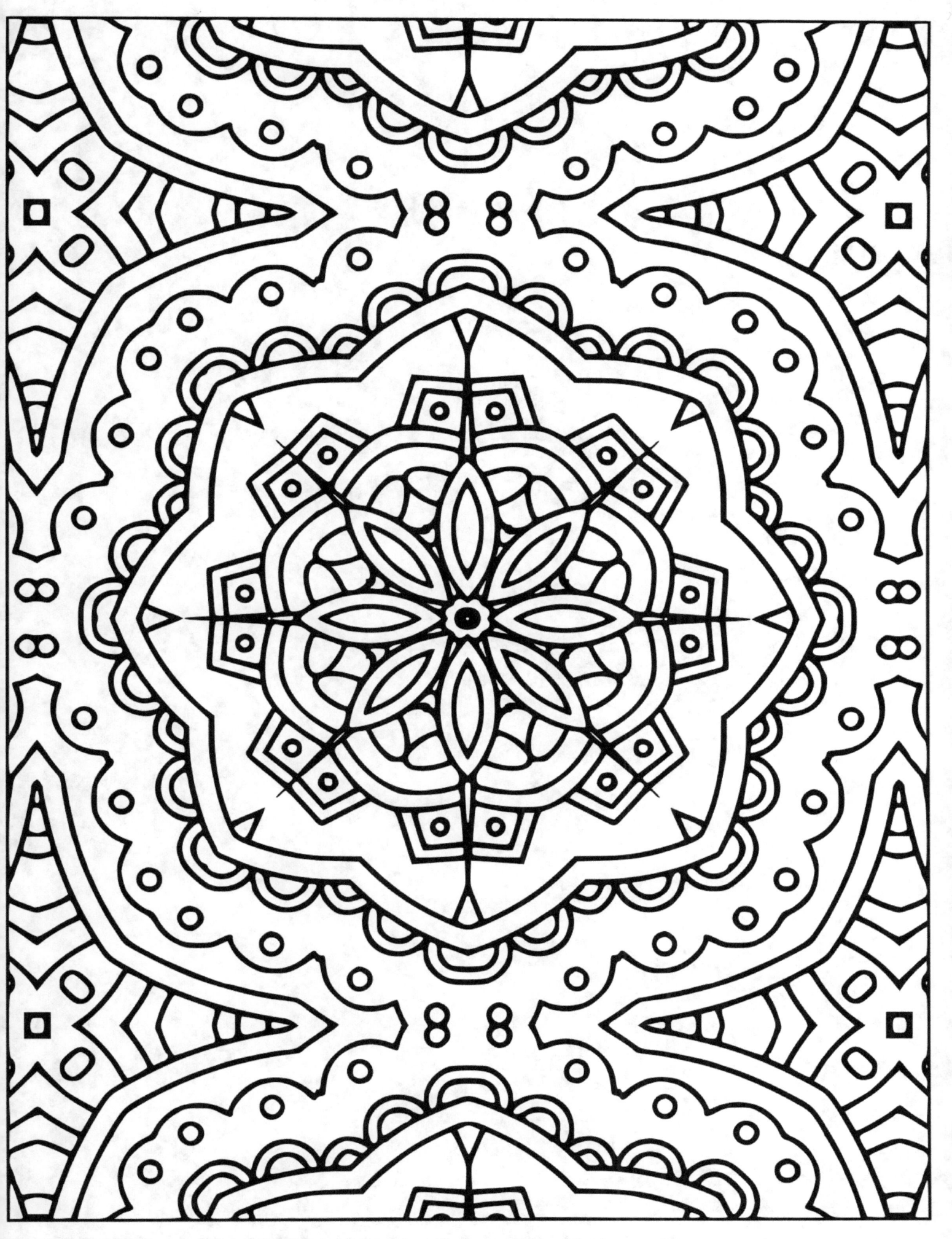

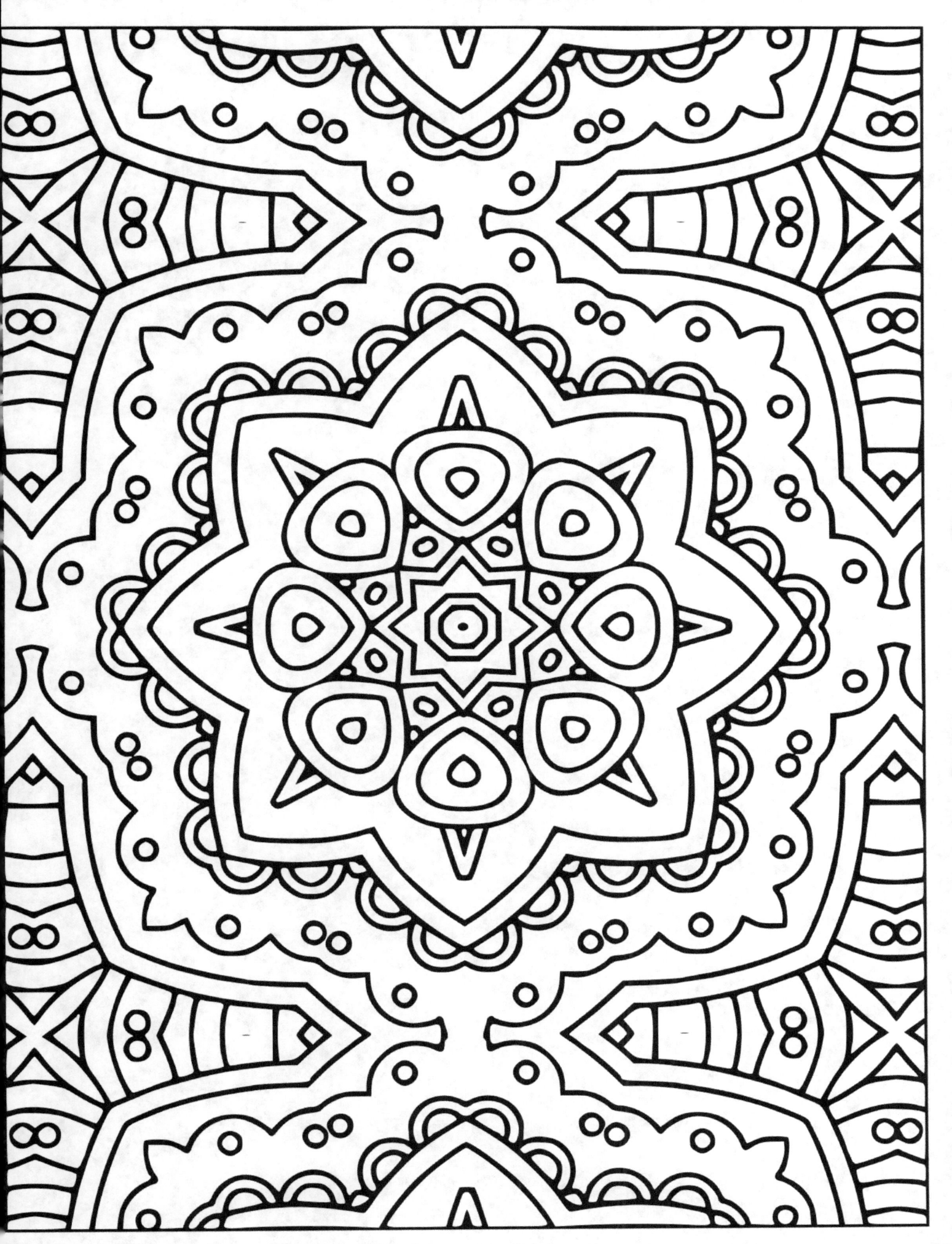

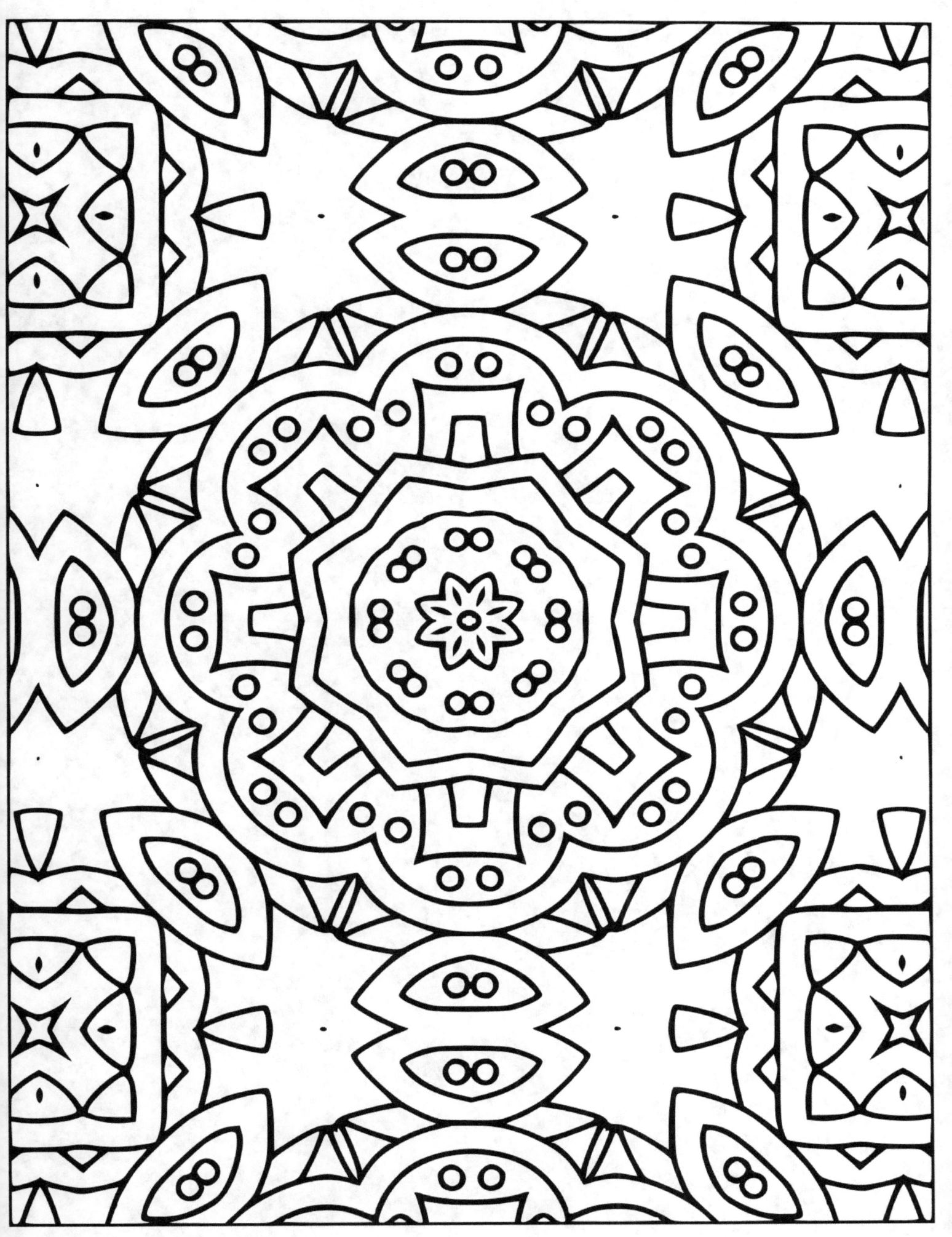

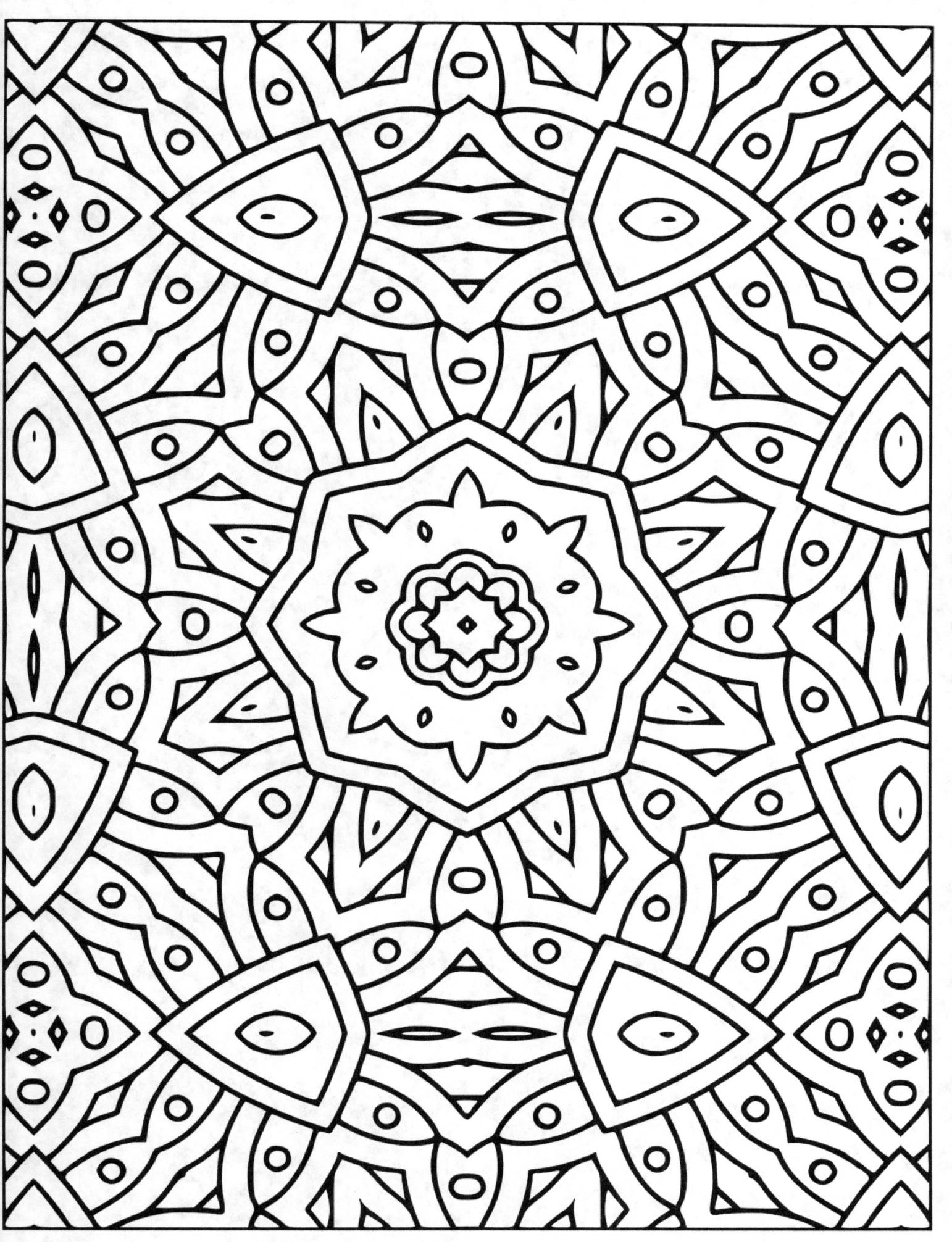

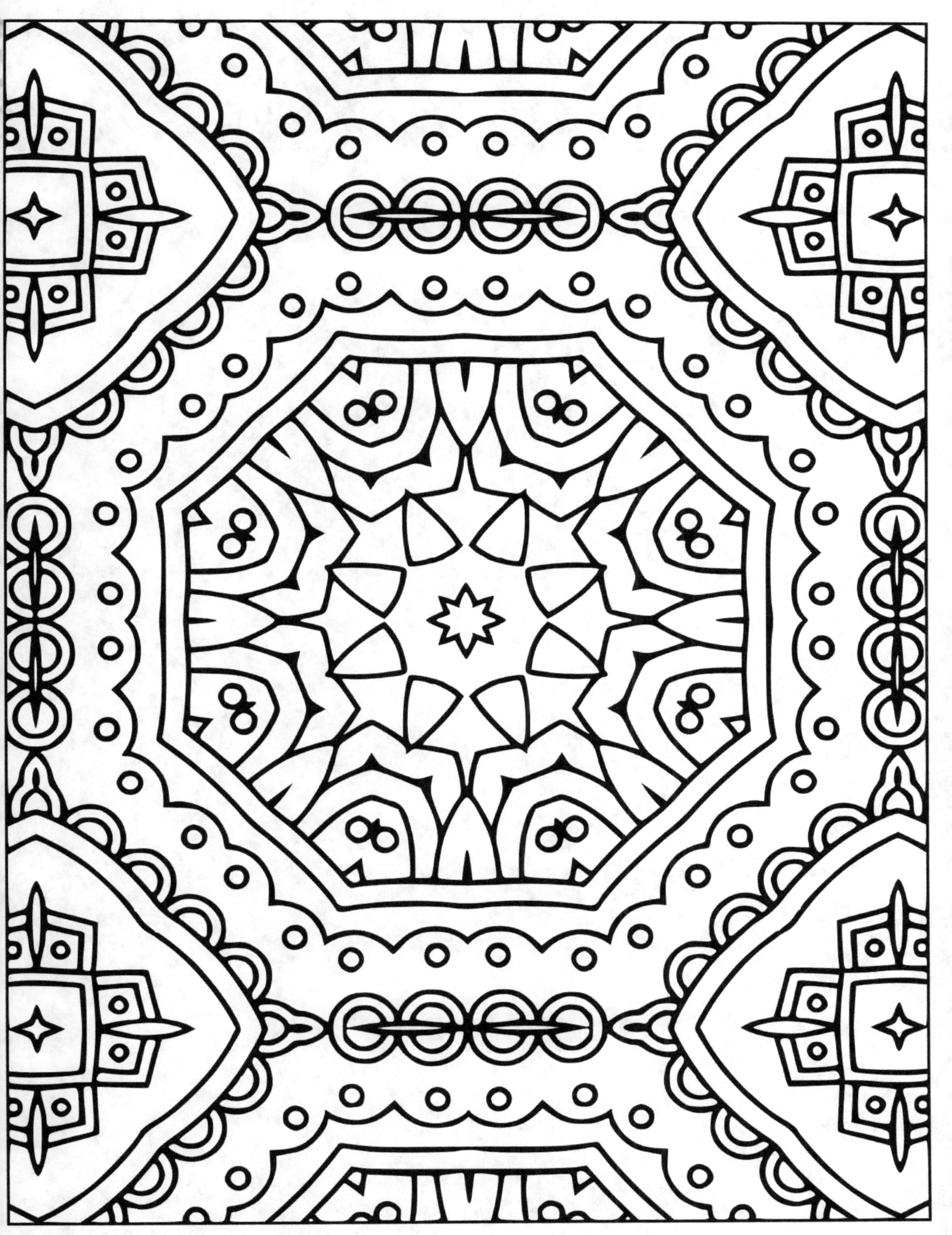

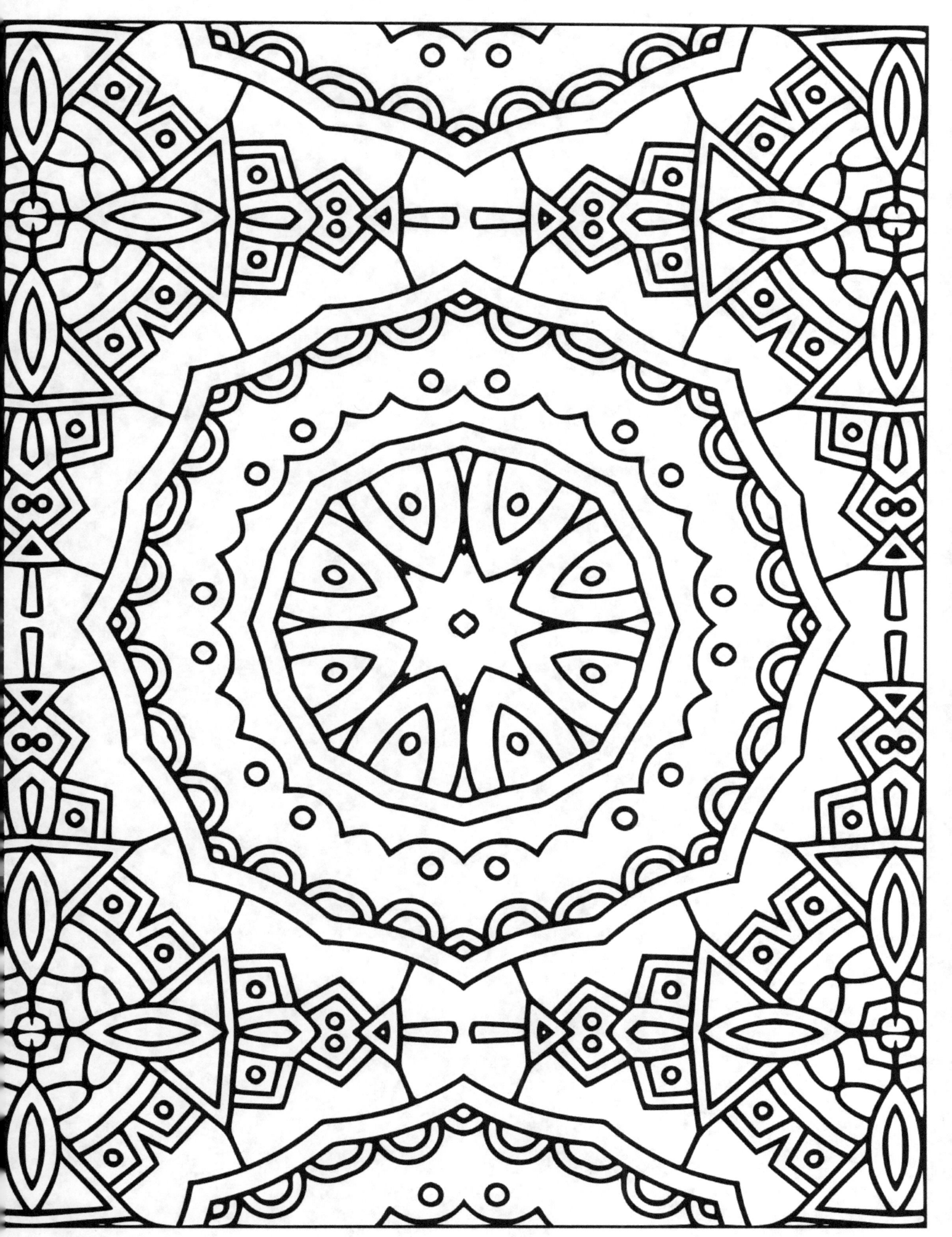

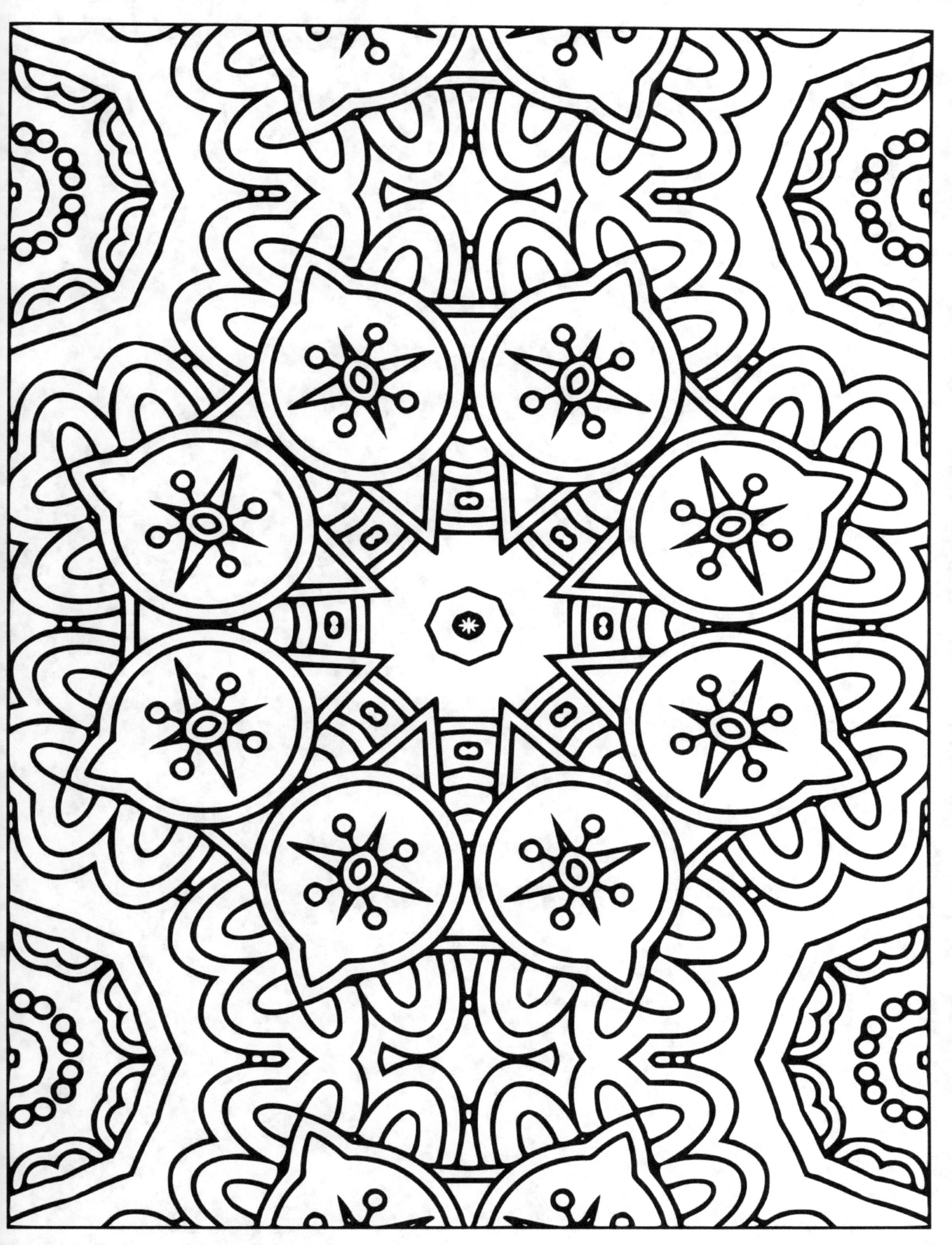

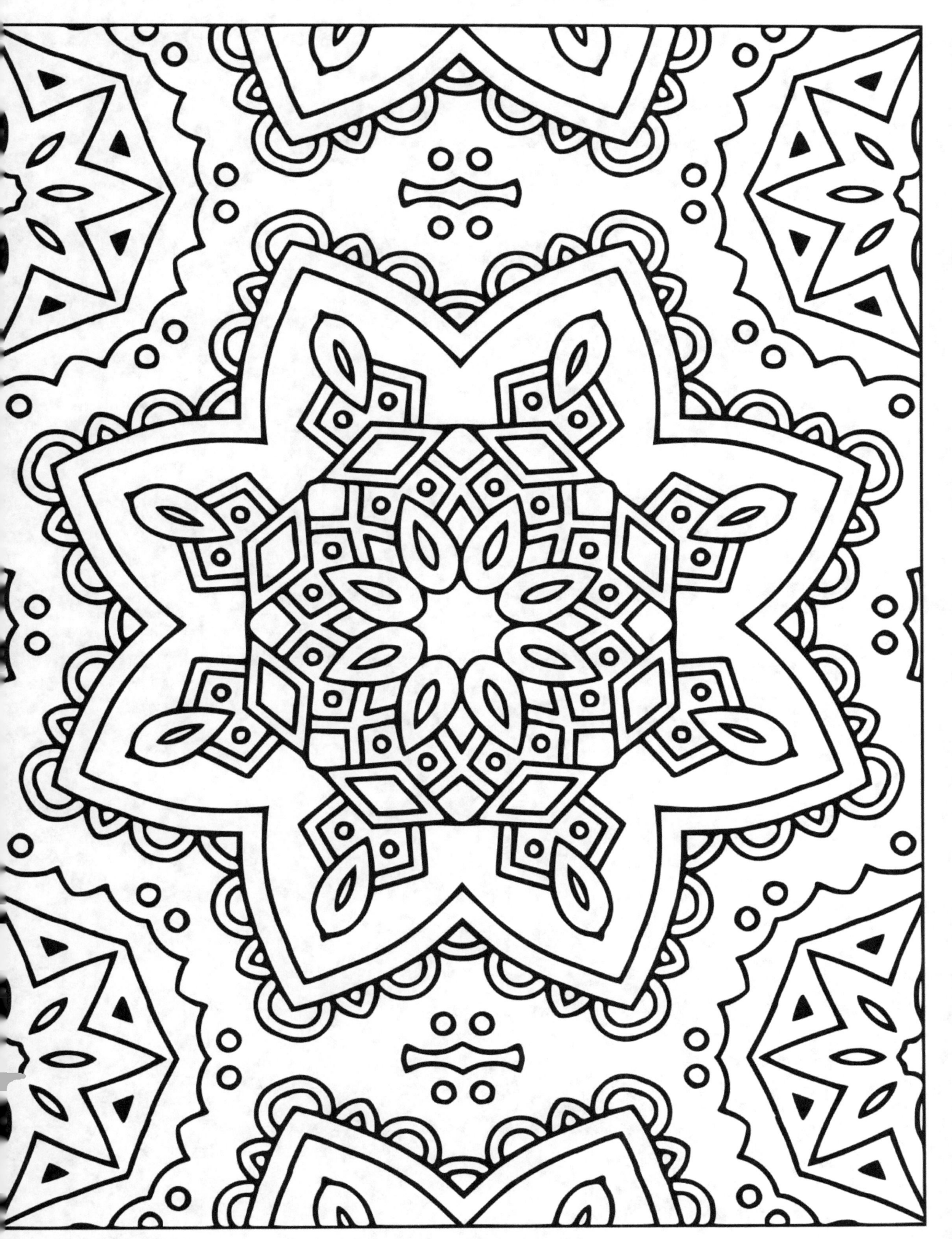

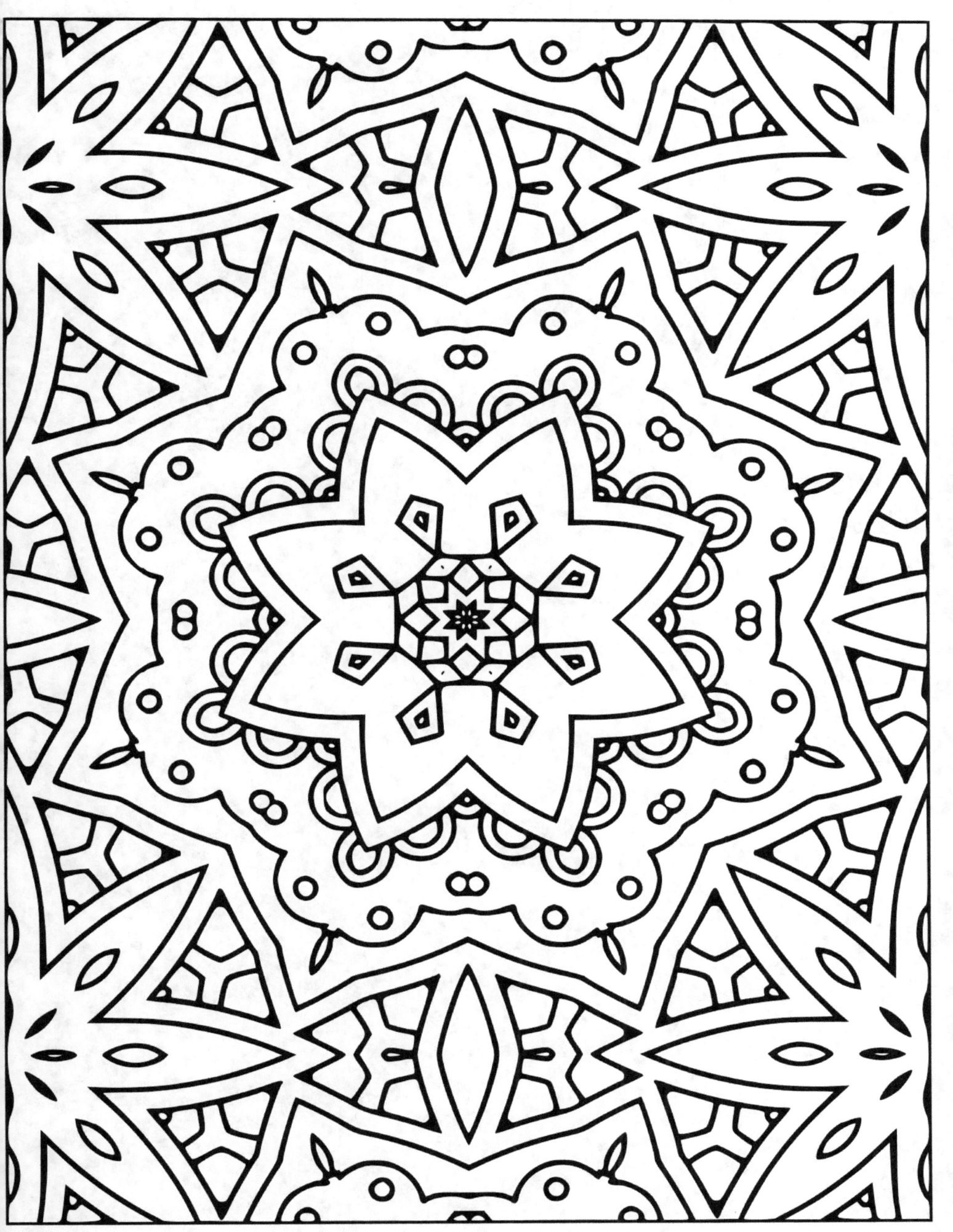

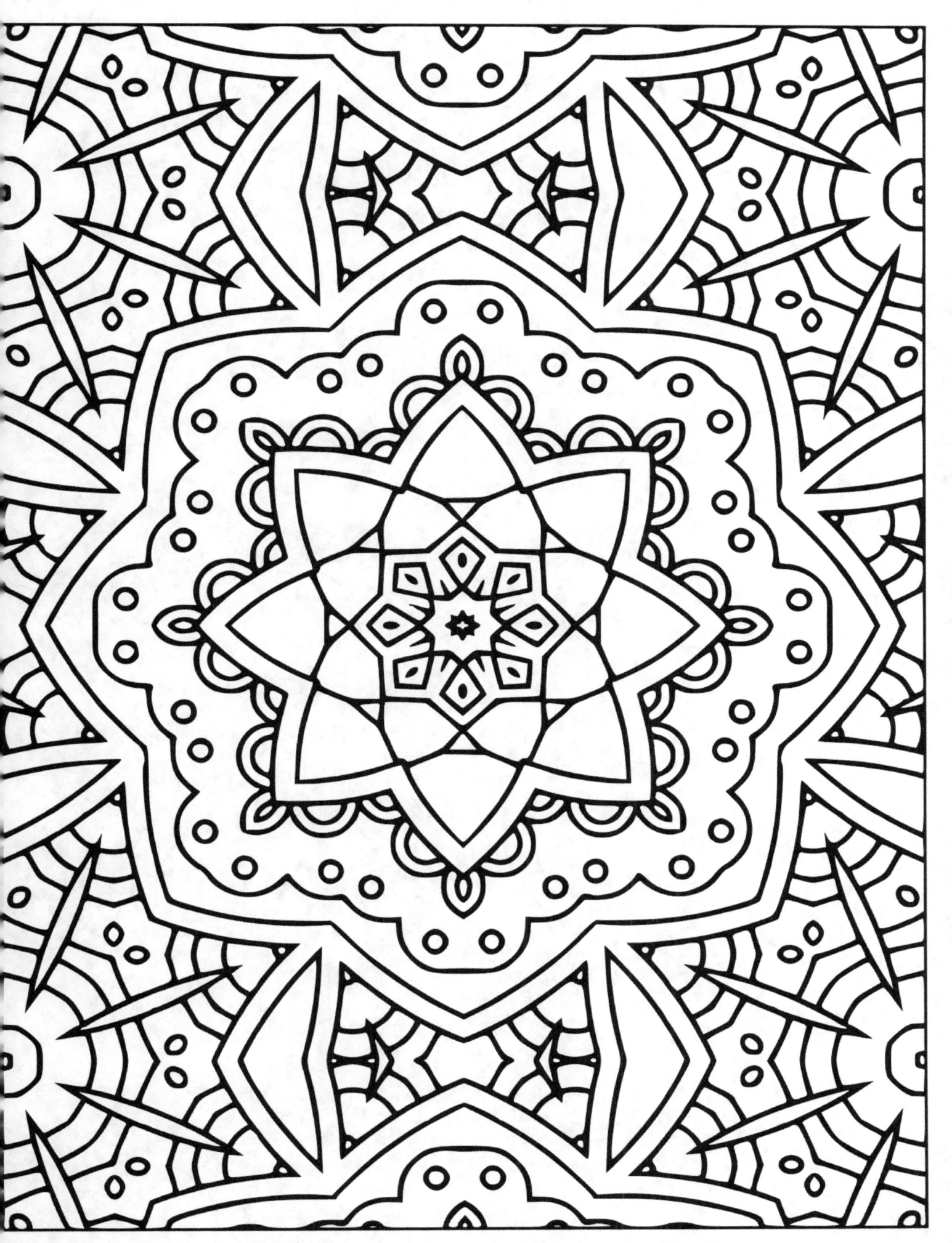

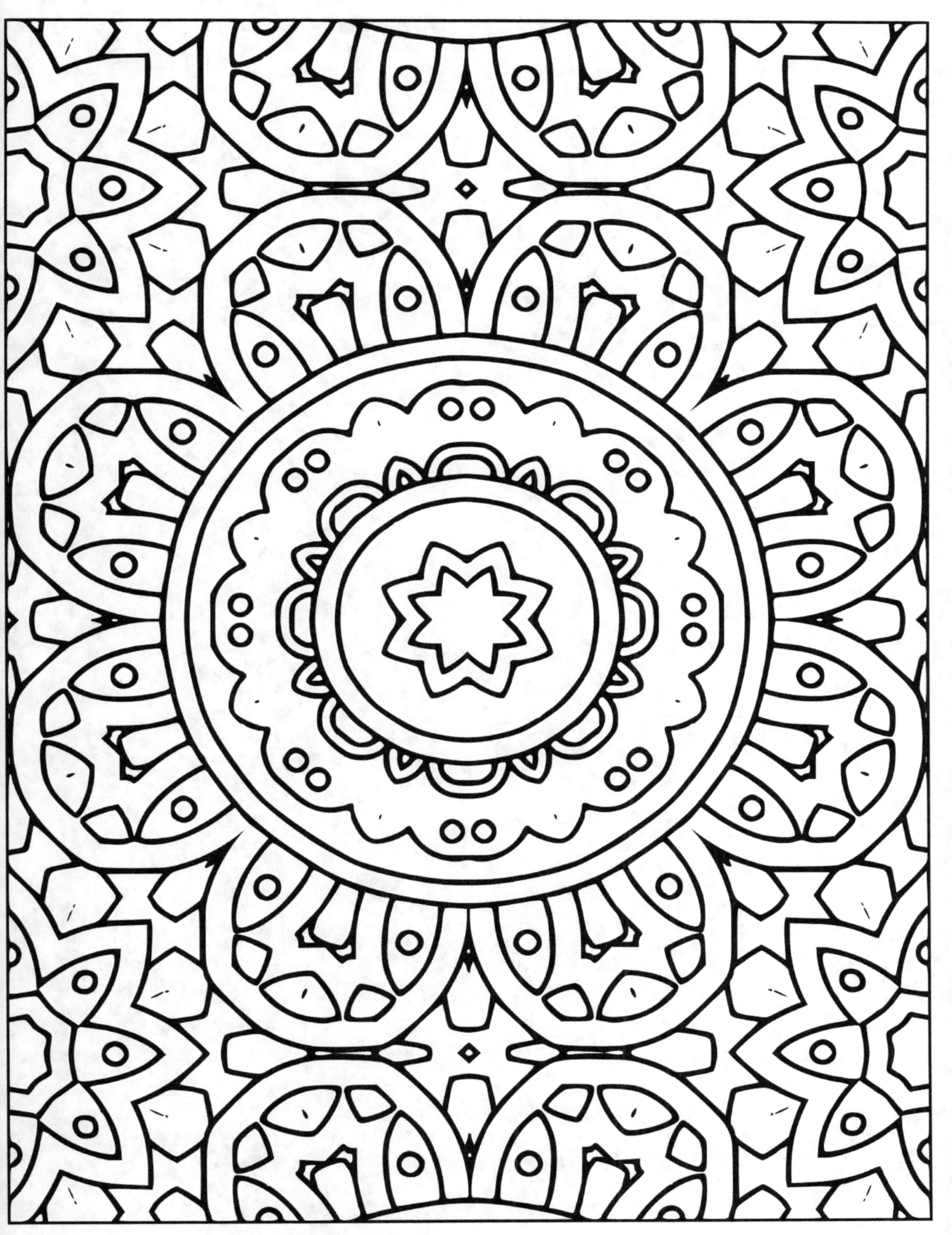

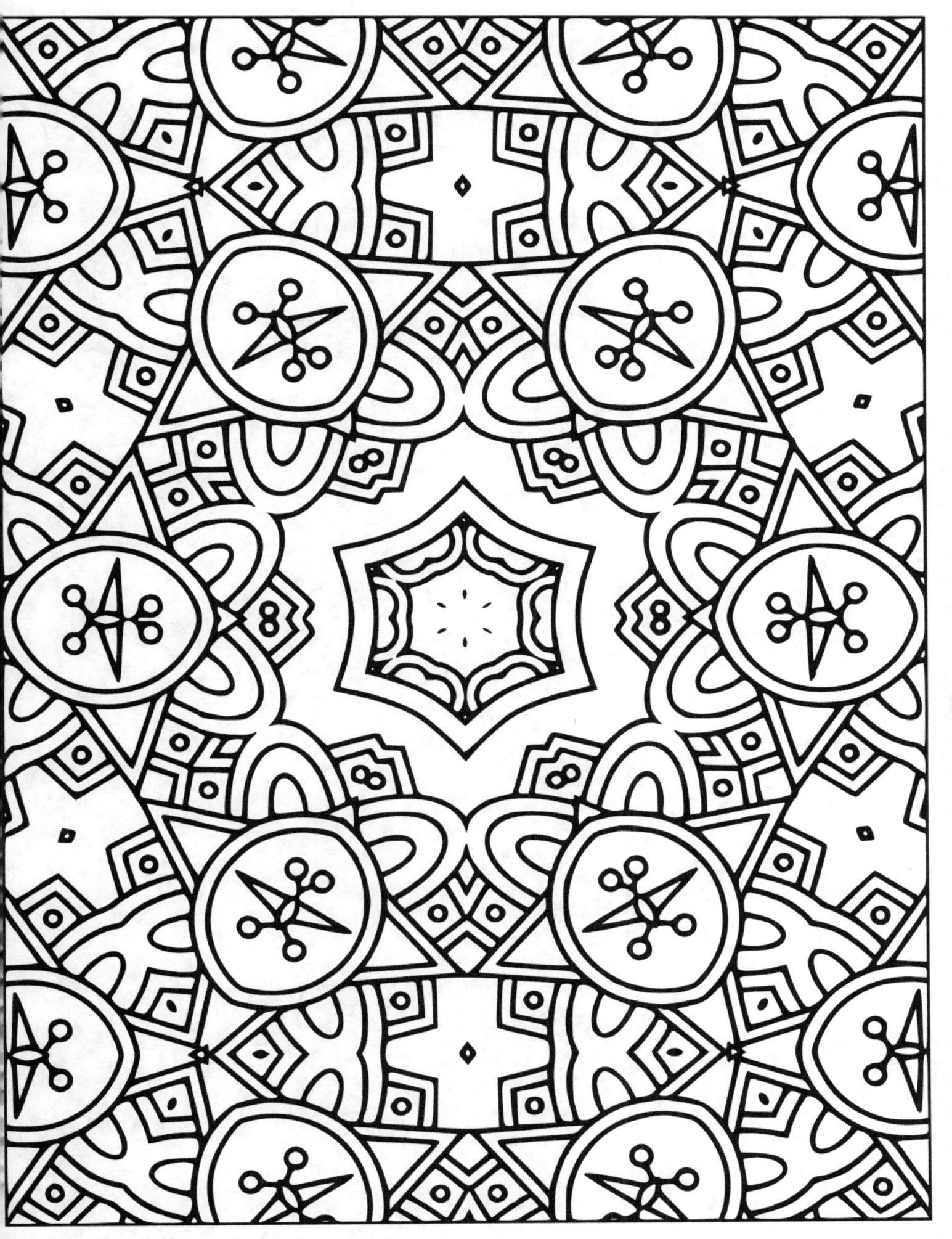

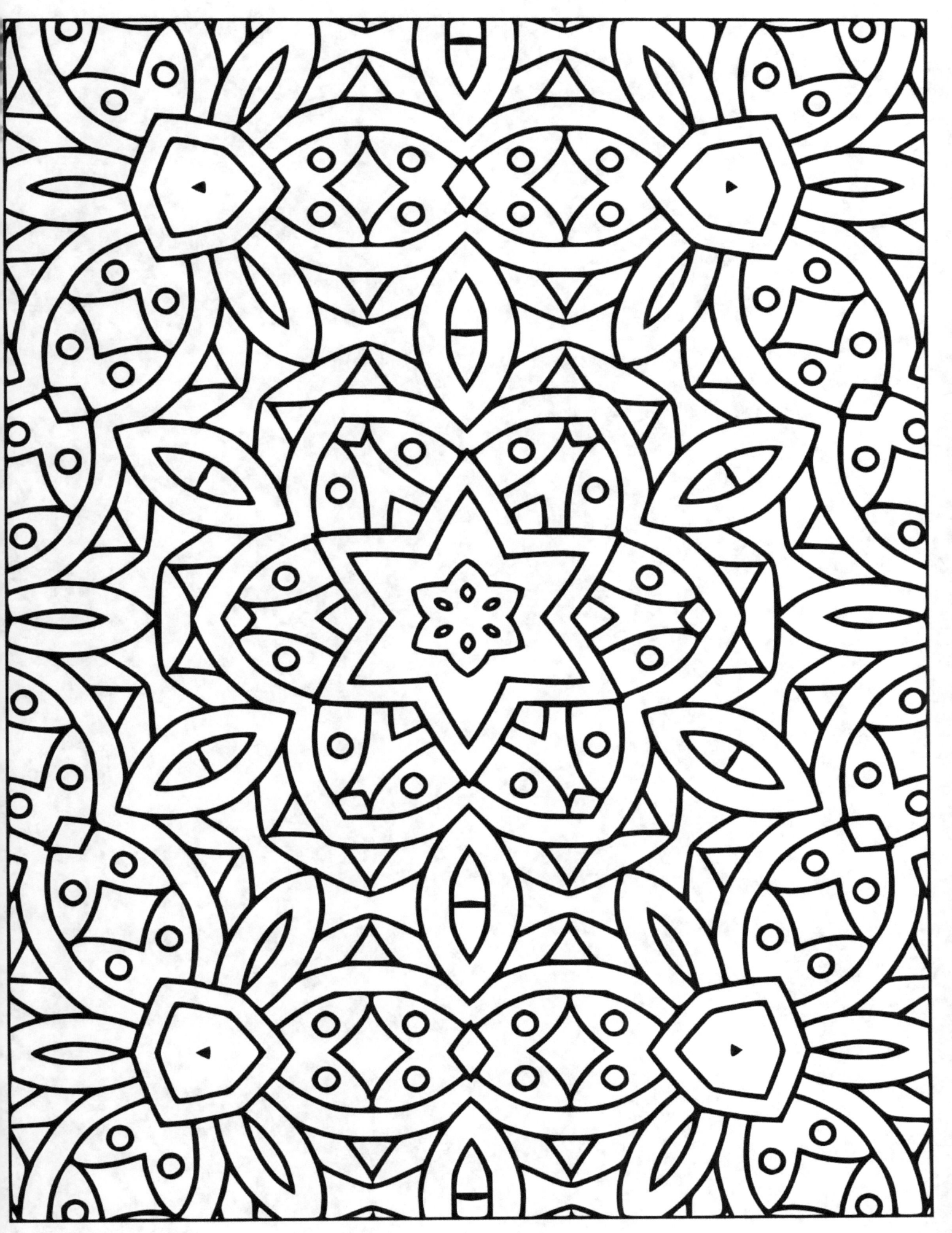

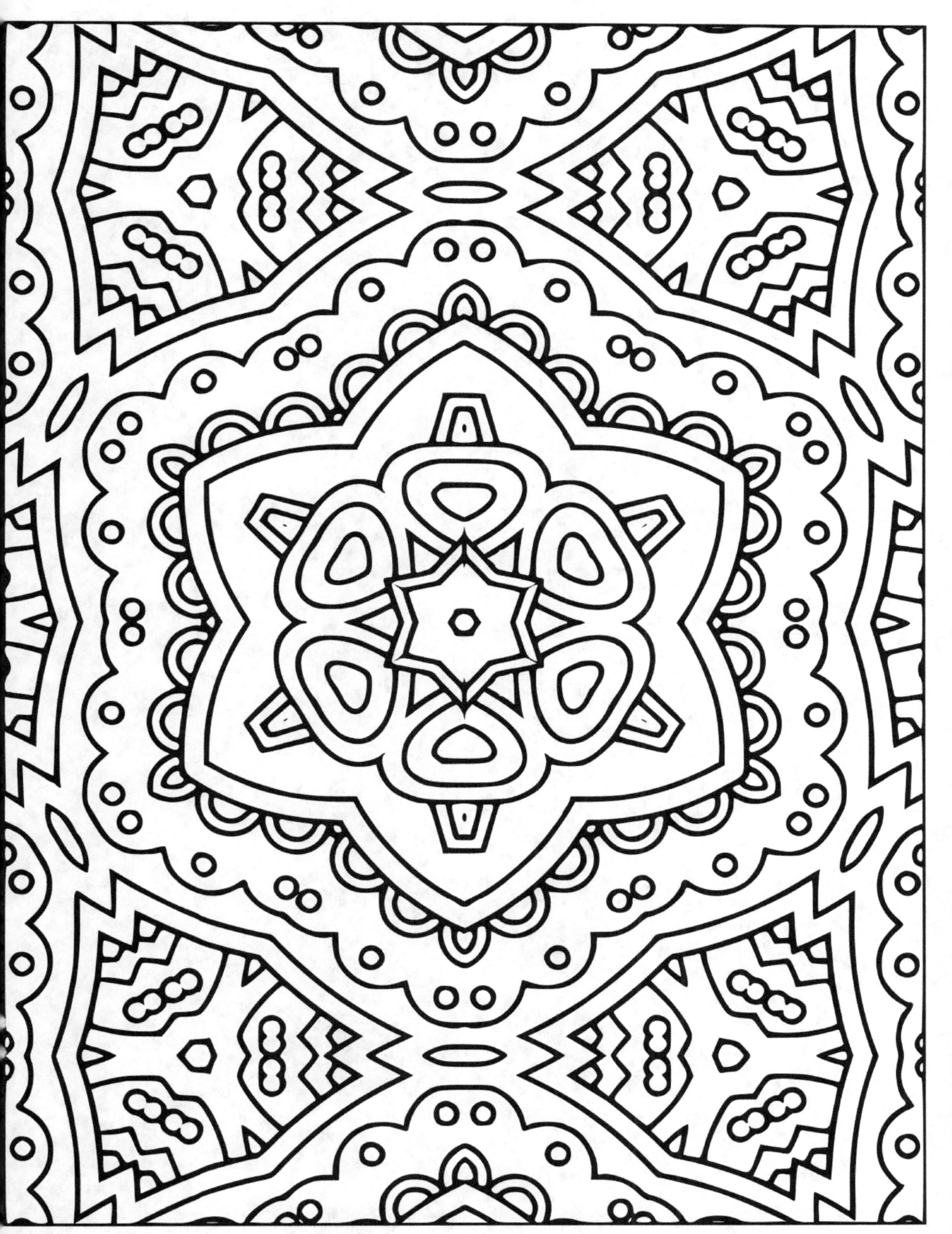

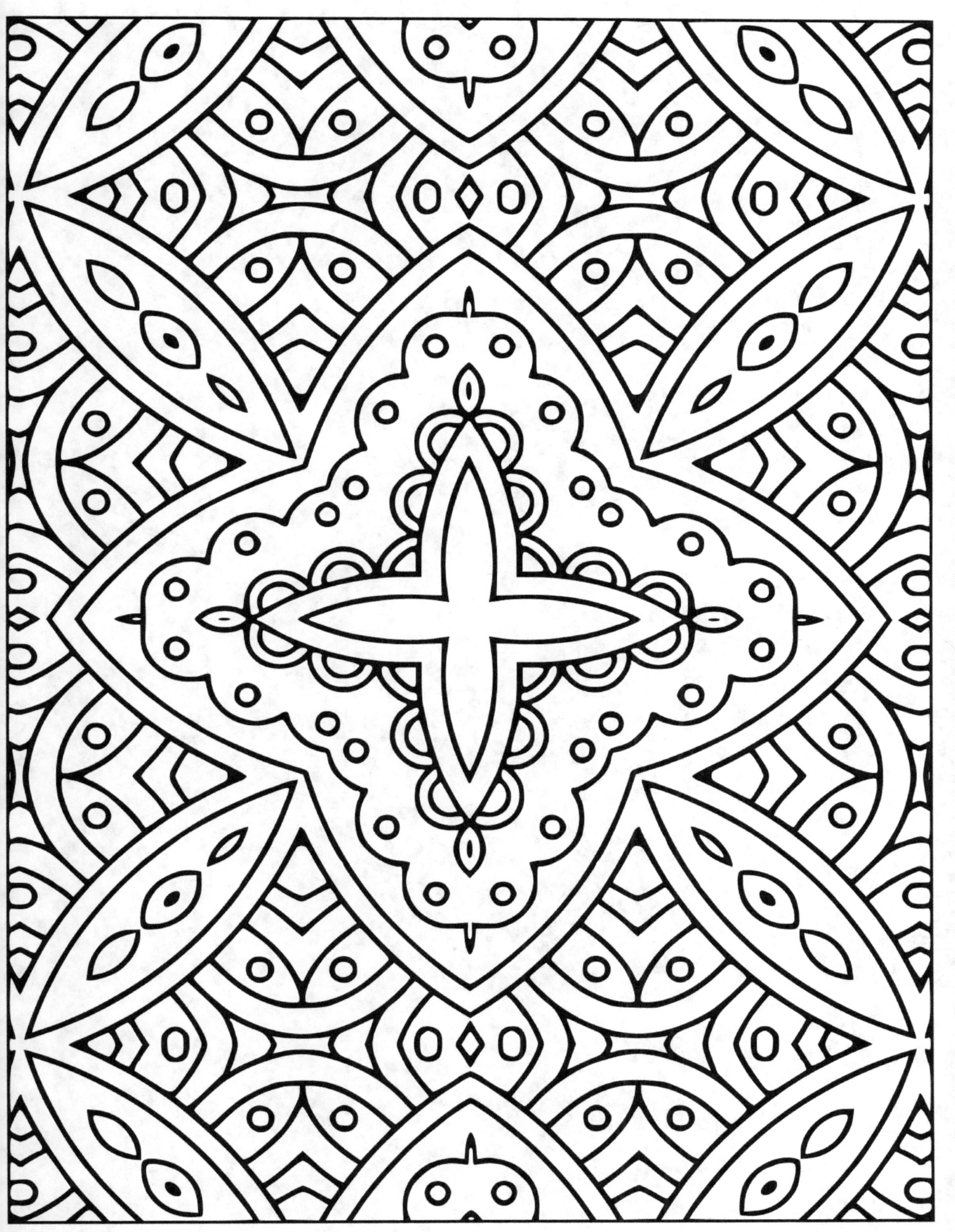

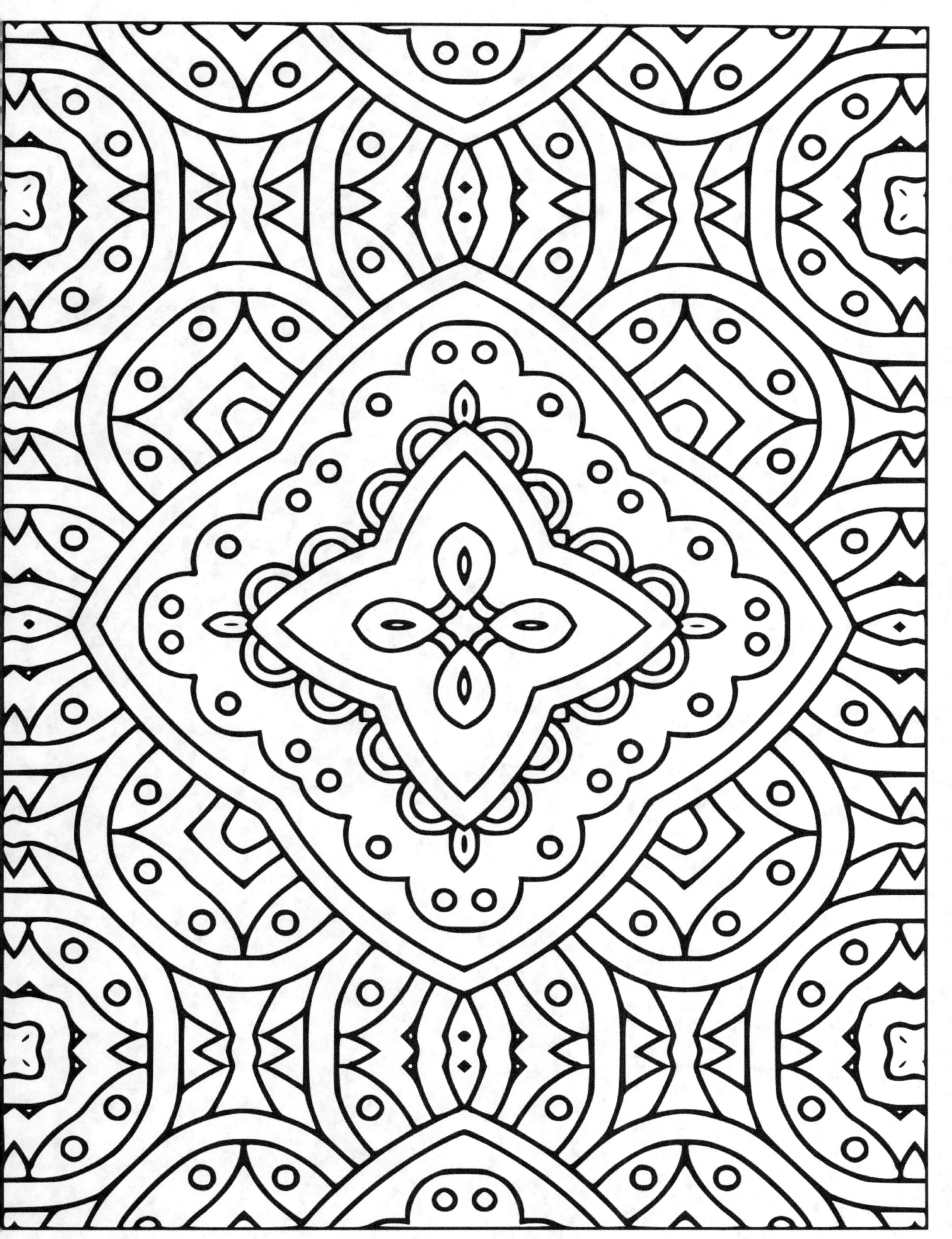

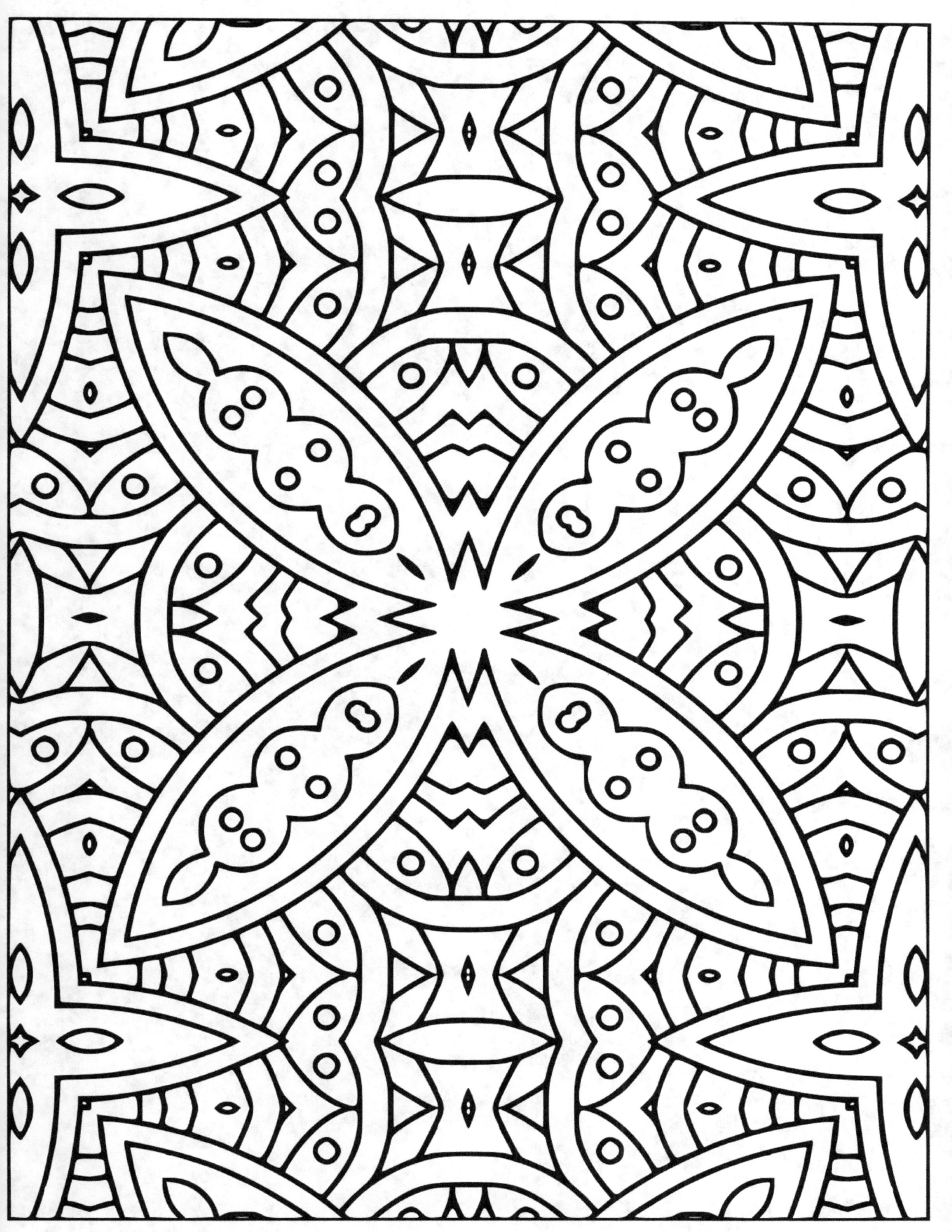

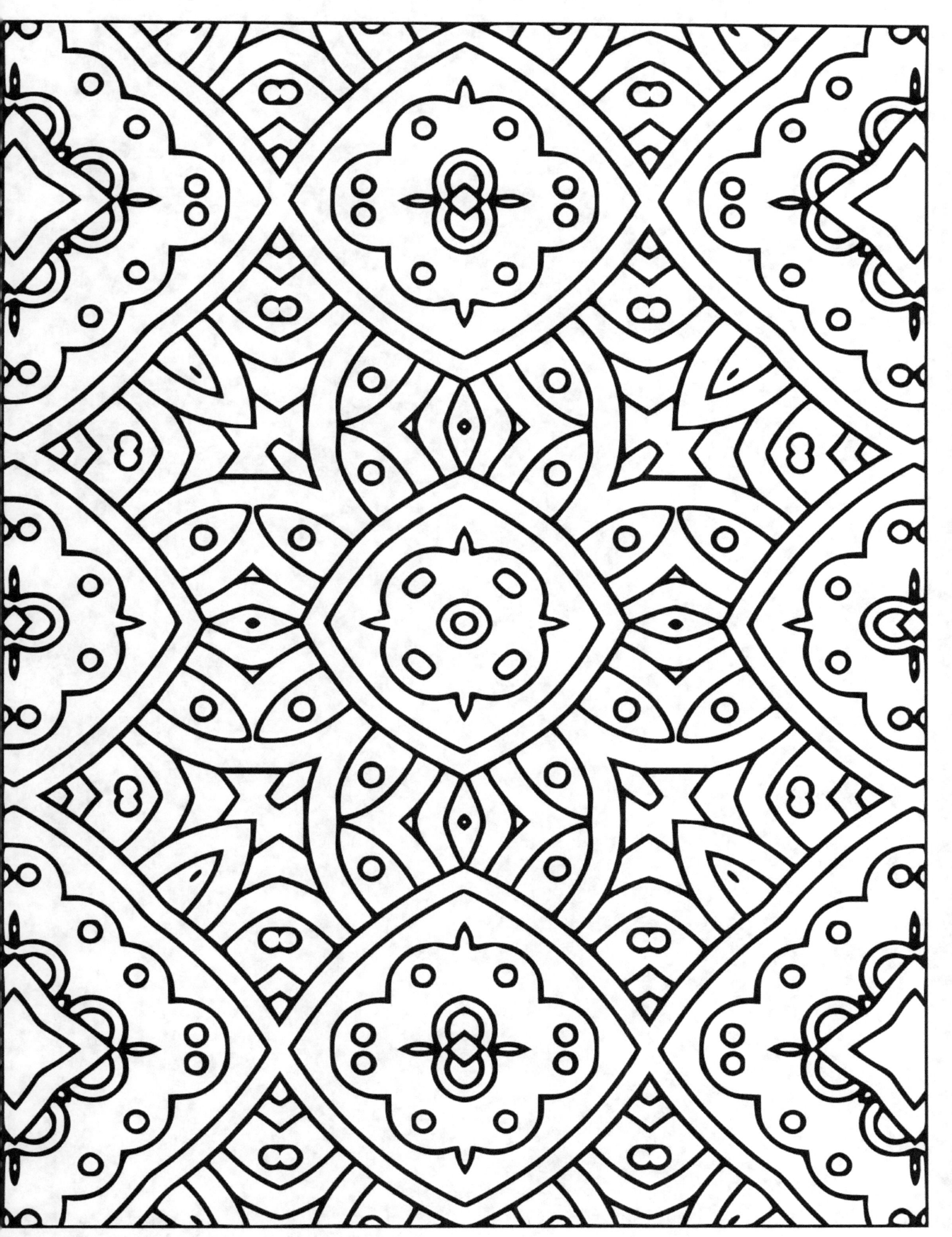

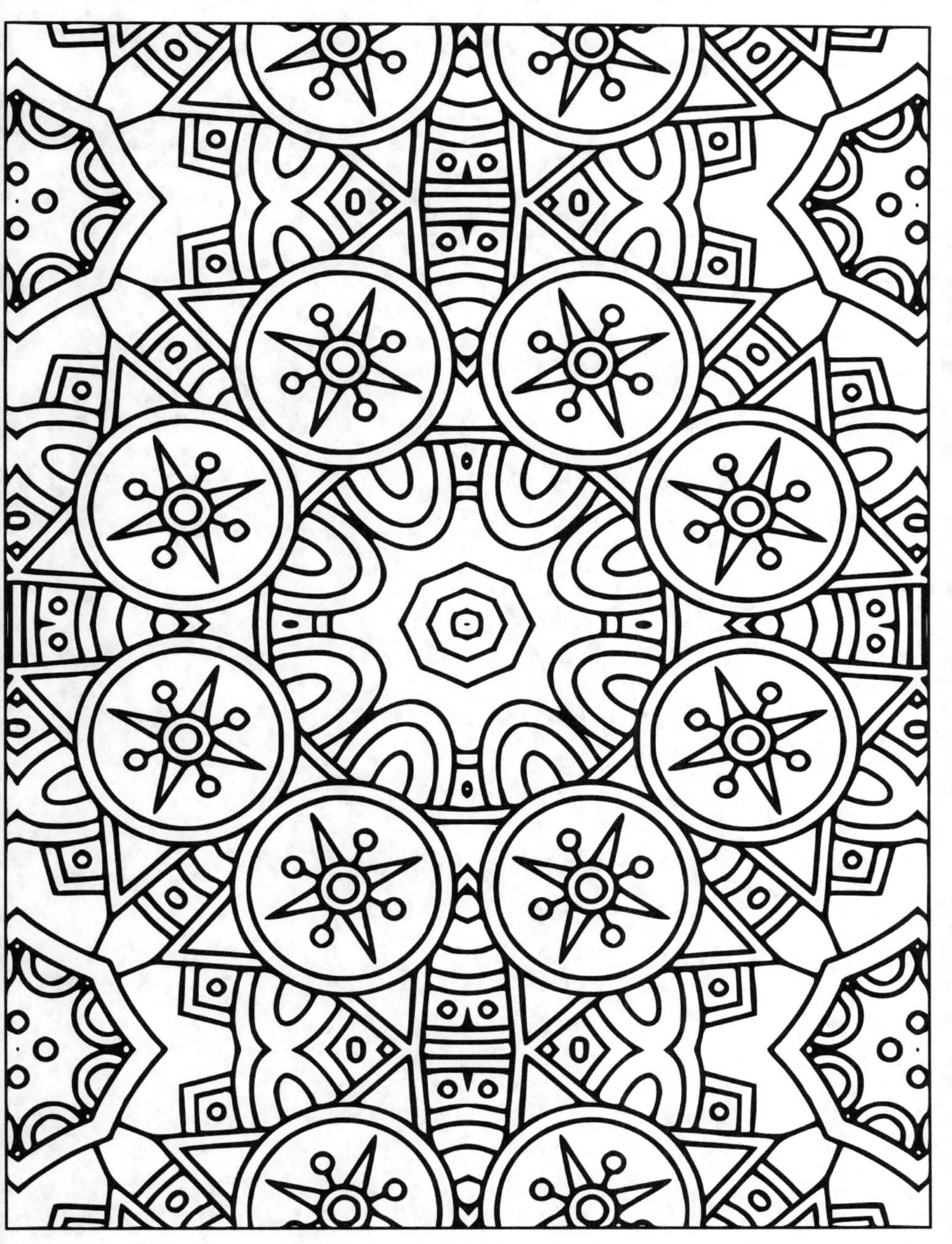

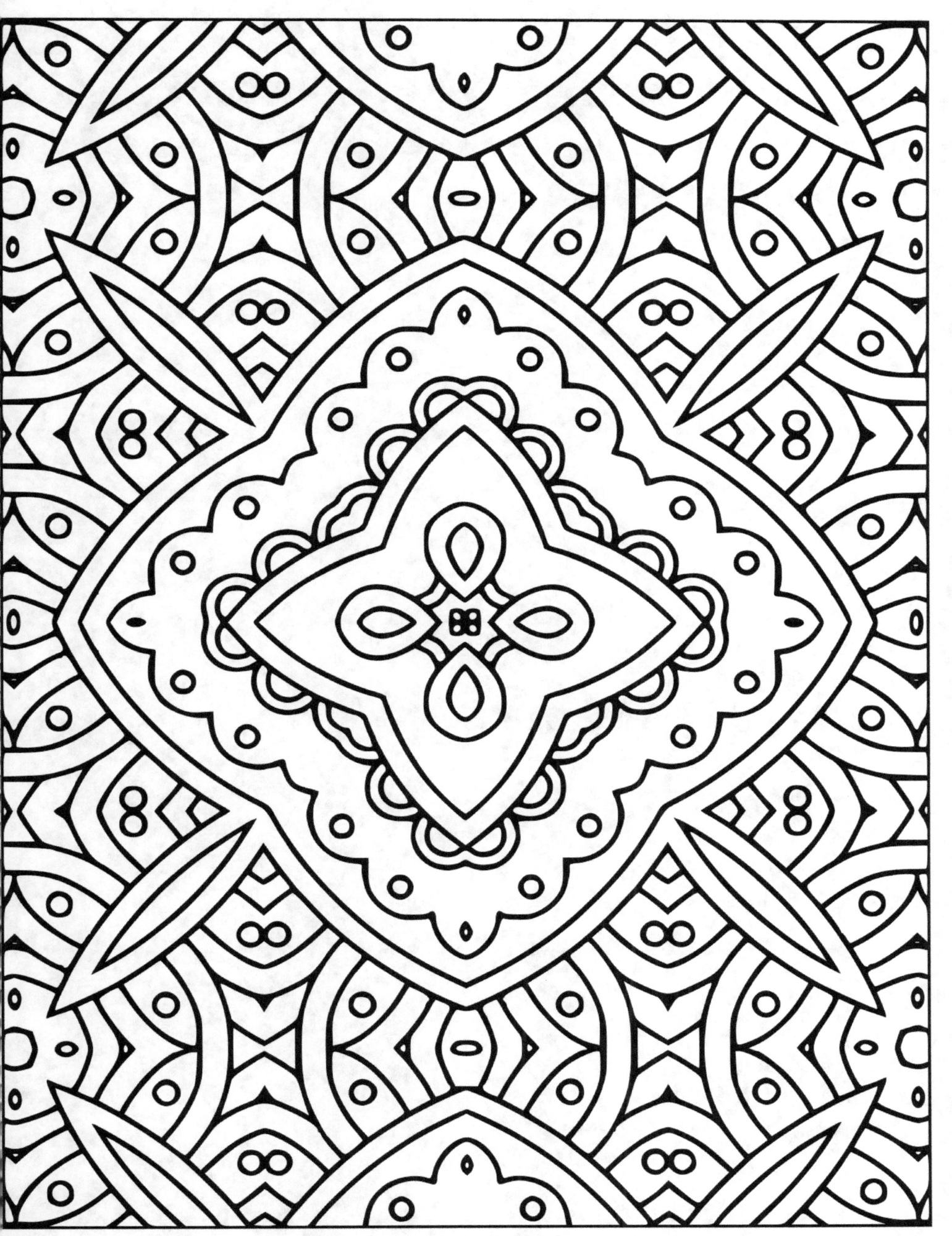

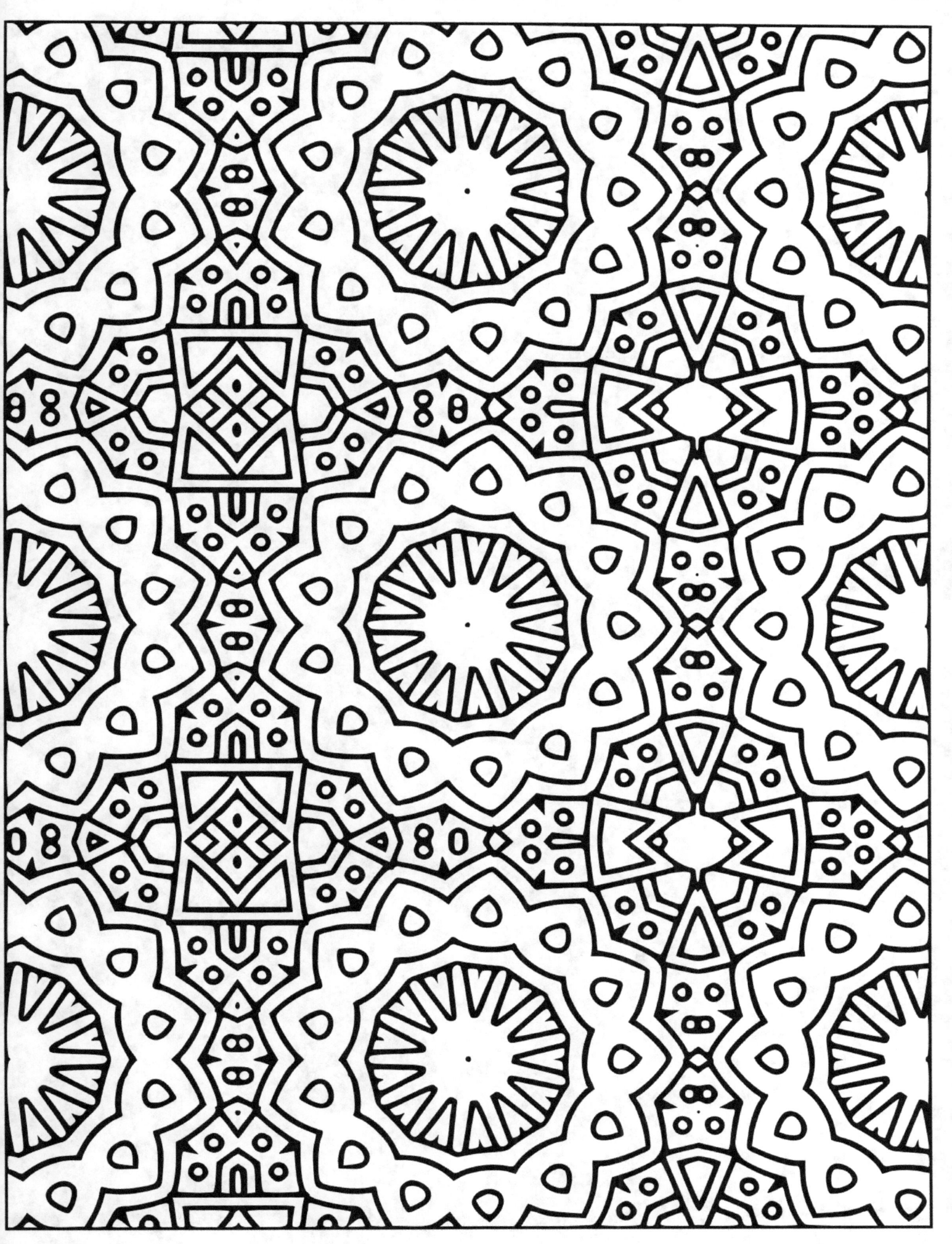

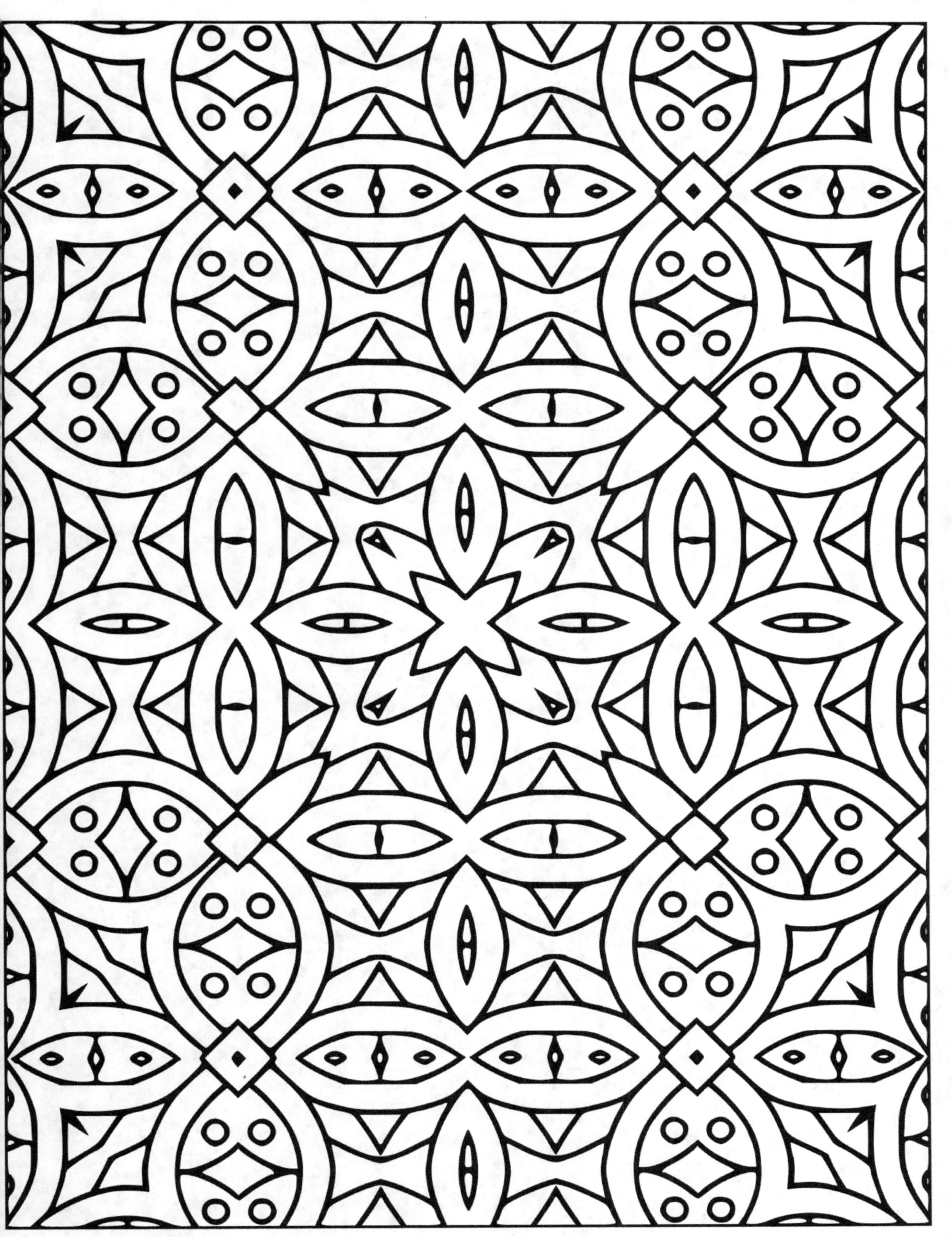

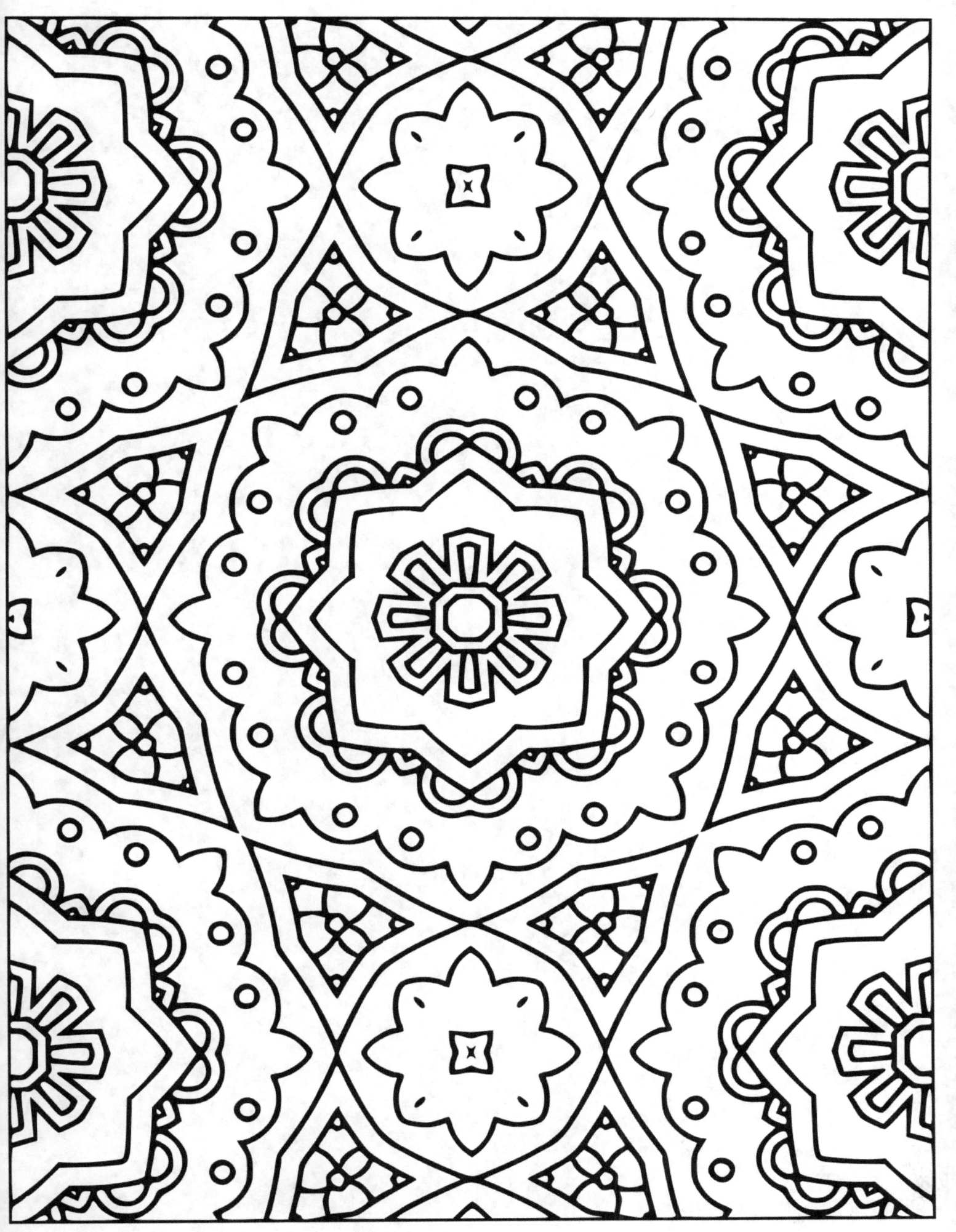

www.ingramcontent.com/pod-product-compliance
Lightning Source LLC
Chambersburg PA
CBHW060437220526

45465CB00008B/3181